Gun Dogs & Bird Guns
A Charley Waterman Reader

Gun Dogs & Bird Guns
A Charley Waterman Reader

Charles F. Waterman

Illustrations by Fred W. Thomas

1986
GSJ Press
South Hamilton, Massachusetts

International Standard Book Number 0-9609842-4-0
Library of Congress Catalog Card Number 86-83012
Printed in the United States of America
Published by GSJ Press
205 Willow Street
South Hamilton, Massachusetts 01982

DEDICATION

For my wife, Debie, who has put up with all this foolishness
for all these years.

Introduction

I sometimes think that it would be possible to live a full and rich life in the outdoors without ever lacing up a boot, uncasing a shotgun, heeling a bird dog or trying to shoot a bobwhite quail. You could have a treasure house of remembered sunrises, cold feet, wet hands, full and empty game bags, unruly pointers, fine companions and covey flushes in rimrock, palmetto thicket and sun-dappled alder run, each stored away in a loose packing of laughter tied together with an occasional teardrop, and you could have them without ever leaving a city apartment.

All you'd have to do is to read Charley Waterman.

Charley's sense of what counts out there, of what's funny, or absurd, or touching, or truly irreducible out there is so apt, so resonant that, for those of us who have read much of his work, it is difficult sometimes to separate what we learned afield from what Charley told us in a sporting magazine some years before. We no longer try.

I hope that you are at least partially among us, that Charley's work is not new to you, and that you are looking forward to these twenty-five pieces as part of the continuum. If so, then you're probably already tapping your fingers on the page, ready to get on to the real stuff, the Waterman stuff. Okay.

But if Charley is new to you, well. . . Welcome.

Ed Gray

Contents

Gun Dogs & Bird Guns
A Charley Waterman Reader

A successful outdoor writer is one who fishes and hunts all he wants to and is able to exist on what he sells. So I have made it. With some embarrassment I confess that I would just as soon write as fish or hunt and I am perpetually amazed that anyone pays me for the stuff.

Chapter One

Success Story

I am exactly what I wanted to become when I was seven years old. Since 7-year-olds are not noted for mature judgment and sometimes aspire to piracy or gunfighting, this is not necessarily a pinnacle of success. The fact is that I have had other goals at various times during the intervening years, most of which I never achieved. Some of those I reached didn't amount to much.

I was raised on a farm in southeastern Kansas. Note that I do not use the term "grew up" since I never seemed to manage that. Farm work didn't appeal to me but I don't think the problem was laziness. Maybe if we'd had a tractor I would have liked to farm.

Midwest hunting and fishing wasn't too much when I was getting started. In 1913, when I was born, southeastern Kansas, like much of the country, hadn't seen a deer for years. They were not the good old days and the drill was to shoot most of what moved. A coyote sighting mobilized the community. There were some prairie chickens a few miles away but I never saw one.

Because of a mother's iron whim I learned to read when I was two years old and acquired a passionate love for a 1914 copy of *National Sportsman*. After that, I read all sporting magazines I could get my hands on, pursued sunfish and bullheads and trapped skunks, opossums and muskrats along Cow Creek. I shot some rabbits and missed some quail. In high school I was too young and too small for most athletics, starting at eleven and barely making the track team as a senior. I had discovered the smallmouth rivers of the Ozark Mountains and in summer I camped along James River when I should have been at home working. I am truly ashamed that in an industrious farming community I was something of a disgrace and a burden to my father. I wasn't bad, just useless. Beginning with a two-dollar bamboo fly rod I was stuck with fly fishing for the rest of my life, but when I was twenty-something I got my first good rod through a man named Russell Francis, who ran a fly-making shop in Pittsburgh, Kansas, of all places.

I learned the opinion of me held by real farmers when I came home from college one summer and "pitched in the field" during wheat harvest. The pitchers forked bundles to the wagons that took them to the big separator and it seemed we were a little short-handed. Anyway, I got no rest at all, the long day bringing me an unbroken file of empty racks while other pitchers managed some rest. Of course it was automatically rigged to "kill the college kid." "Kill" was the indelicate term used to mean wear out to the point of collapse. I made it through the day, calling on all the gristle and grunt I'd learned on a wrestling mat at school, and when I came in as the machine shut down I used my last reserve. Pretending I was in a hurry to get home, I *ran* to my Model A while my tormentors watched in rueful disappointment. I barely made the running board but I never let it show.

When I'd gotten through college (D-minuses in Latin and A's in Literature [honest]) it was the Great Depression and I found myself teaching in a country school briefly. I sold my Harley Davidson and did some professional wrestling. In those days there was pro work for a 160-pounder but I never made more than expense money and I guess wrestling was compensation for my lack of athletics in school. Juvenile. Pro wrestling was much the same then as it is today—without the funny costumes. I got acquainted with some famous wrestlers of the day and found that the "heels" (wrestling parlance for villains) were nearly always very nice guys. I wrestled around some carnivals and concluded that the hardest knockers of all were those who traveled with the carneys and wrestled or fought all comers. In winter, some of those carney fellows were big time showmen with other names.

Then I became a newspaper reporter, wearing my hat in the house and working on some Kansas dailies and weeklies. I decided photography was the coming thing and became a photographer on the side with my eyes on *Life Magazine*. *Life* did not look back at me. I wrote my first outdoor column in 1934 but got no extra pay for it. The publishers considered such stuff frivolous and deserving no paid space in a real newspaper. I was trying to sell to the pulp westerns and couldn't. A reporter sitting across a desk from me had gone big with science fiction and his reporter's pay was just a little extra when he wasn't really working. I sold nothing.

When I went to war I was into the Navy as a Third Class Photographer's Mate, taught Navy photography for a while at Pensacola and ended up the head of a combat photo team in the Pacific, a little late for most of the biggest battles but in the unusual position of being able to travel all over the ocean as a marginal viewer of war. Although our stuff was motion pictures and stills for use in news media, some of the Navy brass were still unable to understand war coverage, feeling pretty sailors with shiny shoes were the only usable subjects. The best stuff I photographed was while on a PT boat that was hit by a Japanese shore battery. Nothing ever came of those pictures and I found them in the Navy Department in Washington when I got home from the war. They had never been released to the press because I did not have the names of the wounded. I was lucky to know the name of the island the shells came from, and now I've forgotten that, but it was in the Philippines. Still, not all of our pictures were lost in the bureaucratic shuffle and I still see one occasionally in a war history.

So I came home from the wars and did news photography around San Francisco for seven years and fished or hunted when I could, still throwing bass bugs on impoundments and catching some trout in the Sierras. There were ducks and geese in northern California but there were a lot of people. I had a furious period of competitive pistol shooting and learned I'd never be too good at it, and one day a smallmouth bass stormed up from a riffle in a California river to take what I'd shown him and I was suddenly homesick for some place where the fishing and hunting were close by. My wife Debie and I ended up in 1952 in northern Florida where there were quail, snipe, ducks and whitetail deer and, at the time, little prospect of crowding. If we'd known Disney World was on the way we'd have gone somewhere else.

A couple of magazines folded under us and I kept stabbing blindly at outdoor writing, fighting for every sale, but one day in New York a magazine editor said he'd buy a whole list of stuff and I realized I had arrived—not as a big-time writer but as a freelancer who could sell what he wrote, and I went back to the Wentworth Hotel mad as hell because I could write no better than I could have written 20 years earlier. It had taken a long time. I hadn't been a very good salesman for myself but now I was what I'd wanted to be when I was seven years old and I have been it ever since.

A writer had a free ticket to some extent and I could hunt and fish with good guides all over the world but there appeared an unexpected fly in the soup. I found, somewhat to my consternation, that we wanted to do things on our own and fretted a little when someone else handled the dogs or scoped the sheep. We spent some months every year learning the saltwater Everglades country, using a houseboat part of the time and house trailers part of the time. And we got hooked on Montana, where we began spending several months every year, clear back in the late fifties. At first we lived in apartments and then we bought a little 4-room house. We had one apartment for a number of years at $35 a month.

There was always a bird dog or two to tie us down a little and other writers made more money while they traveled the whole world. With us, trips out of the country were unusual and inclined to be brief. We knew where the Hungarian partridge were in Montana and we had a few quail in Florida, and we made stops in between. Gradually we got out of the big game business and stuck with the birds. I'd had a passion for sheep hunting.

Upland birds bothered me, there were so many kinds, and I found that too many upland gunners tended strongly toward specialization—and when I wrote a book on all of the North American upland birds shot over the same Brittany, I was hooked on a whole list of species. My wife, who had shot in a lot of pistol matches, and had picked off some big muley bucks, stopped at the shotgun.

"I don't have any knack for these things," she said. "I'll go with you and handle dogs but I can't shoot one of these."

I insisted and she tried an over-under twenty-gauge at a practice trap, taking a rifleman's stance despite my dissertation on shotgun technique. She missed her first shot and

tion on shotgun technique. She missed her first shot and when she broke the gun (neglecting to tilt it) the ejector hit her in the face with the empty shell. She said it was an omen and hasn't used a shotgun since. Although she had killed all those deer and antelope and was at home with a rifle or pistol, she still handles a shotgun as if it were a defective bangalore torpedo.

But bird dogs are different. Our bird dogs orbit her, treating me with scornful indifference except during hunting season. She knows all their little problems and converses with them in a sort of pidgin canine. This is not baby talk. They discuss things with her in a series of woofs and wiggles. Dogs have a lot of health problems, ranging from fleas to porcupine quills. I do not talk to veterinarians. Debie does that and while I hold a squirming subject on the inspection table, Debie and the vet carry on a high-level discussion in terms I do not understand. Sometimes it is hard to tell who is prescribing the treatment and I often suspect the vet is more of a supplier than a consultant.

Now Debie, like the wives of most other outdoor scribblers, has been accused of doing the writing, but she doesn't. Debie is a lousy writer and a terrible speller. She is pretty good at photography but she said it was simpler to just put my name on all the pictures, which we do. However, years ago I confessed to someone that she had taken a picture which received extra circulation and she was given an award with her name spelled correctly (Debie instead of Debbie). "Debie" (pronounced *Deebee*) is a contraction of her maiden name, which is Belgian, and she is used to being called "Debbie."

Debie likes to camp more than I do and enjoys cooking meals under adverse conditions. Cowering under a leanto I have watched her doing a number on a driftwood fire, completely unprotected from a snowstorm that sizzled in the skillet. She was humming something from *Oklahoma*. Although I like the surroundings, the work of camping, for me, is just a way of getting outdoors and close to the fish or game. This, I realize, is pretty shaky ground for anyone in my business and I have spent considerable time under canvas, some of which leaked, but my attitude toward camping chores remains about as it was when I used to camp on James River in Missouri. I slept under a tarp and I cooked with kerosene on a rotten stump. When I wanted a fire I doused the stump and lit it. Maybe I would have been taller if the meals had balanced better.

A successful outdoor writer is one who fishes and hunts all he wants to and is able to exist on what he sells. So I have made it. With some embarrassment I confess that I would just as soon write as fish or hunt and I am perpetually amazed that anyone pays me for the stuff. In an ongoing ego that accompanies this wonderment I read everything I've written after it is published, sometimes several times. That's partly because I childishly relive everything I have recounted. This attitude has changed little since my first two paragraphs published in my high school newspaper at Girard, Kansas. When my first book was published I was surprised that it wasn't sold out immediately and I still look it up in libraries once in a while.

It's no trouble for me to sit down to a typewriter and work, even though good writers are supposed to avoid production at all costs. They are supposed to sharpen pencils, read mail and fiddle around the yard to postpone the moment of labor. Also, it seems they are expected to approach the keyboard in an alcoholic haze or write only in the depths of night when the world will not catch them at it. I'd just as soon get at it at 8 A.M., but night is all right too. I found early (roughly 50 years ago) that the only way to freelance is to do it even if the pencils need sharpening and the yard has weeds. I now contemplate the man who mows the yard as he passes my window and I am no longer ashamed that he may make more per hour than I do. Hell, I'm a writer. He's a yard mower and landscaper and probably feels sorry about what appears to be my typewriter enslavement.

I was not that big a success as a war photographer, or a news photographer, or a literature teacher (Stetson University), or a baby photographer, or a farmer, or a wrestler, or a book salesman (I came home on freight trains from Baker, Oregon) or a reporter or an editor. I am an outdoor writer who hunts and fishes and tries to get it on paper and is still a little afraid of magazine editors and I never, never mow the damned yard.

I figured the other day that I hauled bird dogs for 9,000 miles over the main highways last year, indulging in a juvenile tendency to migrate with the bird seasons. After three or four years of that a dog begins to figure what's going on, and although he can't drive himself, he is beginning to think about it.

Chapter Two

On Tour

I t seems we have always traveled with dogs in automobiles. Small dogs in large automobiles work pretty well but large dogs in small cars have presented problems from time to time.

I have no objection to sending bird dogs on airplanes but airplanes don't seem to go where we want our bird dogs to go. There are, of course, little traumas occasionally resulting from aerial dog travel. Our friend Chuck was relaxing in his 727 window seat at a large city airport when he noted a well-conformed English pointer strolling across the runway. After admiring the dog's gait and markings Chuck noted they were familiar and concluded suddenly that the pointer belonged to him, whereupon he charged down the aisle. Chuck is large and his progress was only slightly impeded by the efforts of unprepared flight attendants. Before reinforcements could be mustered he had bellowed his way onto the field and recruited baggage handlers who helped him collect Peaches, who didn't feel the airport appeared to have very good quail cover anyway. It seems her shipping crate had broken when dropped from a baggage truck, much to Peaches' humiliation.

Chuck was not seriously discouraged by this mishap and Peaches showed no aversion to another trip by airline, landing happily at Jackson, Wyoming near some excellent sharptail grouse shooting. Chuck and his twenty-gauge Parker, however, were in Boise, Idaho, where the chukar season was just opening. Chuck chartered a light airplane and managed to get back with Peaches so that they missed only one day of chukars.

But most of the time we and our dogs travel by truck, car or trailer. There have been quite a number of dogs, most of which have shared our bed and board for long periods. Some years ago I fell in with Ben Williams, who raises Brittanies, and made an arrangement whereby I would occasionally contribute to the dog food fund and would have use of his dogs, of which he had quite a number. Although Ben was partial to Brittanies, our personal dogs have been pointers and setters as well. Occasionally we have consorted with Labrador retrievers. Anyway, if it seems we have toured with more canines than normal, this is a partial explanation.

No example of canine intuition is as puzzling to me as their knowledge that a long trip is impending. For example, when I was a kid on the farm we took a week's camping trip by Model T Ford and left our dog in the care of a neighbor. A year later my father began to install his homemade luggage carrier on the car's running board for the second time and the dog crawled under the Ford and howled. Any dog could note a luggage carrier being installed and figure that it meant we were packing up to leave again rather than taking eggs to town. Nothing remarkable about that, I guess.

But at our house, when we begin to discuss a coming trip there is a sudden restlessness among the dogs. Maybe not as strong a feeling as when we actually pack a suitcase but a special attitude nevertheless. Of course once we drag out a couple of duffel bags the fat is in the fire. We had one dog who would then bark until we allowed him to load up in the car. He would relax there, temporarily confident he was not going to be left behind. If we packed a day before leaving we'd have to drag him out of the car for the night. Dogs are dumber than we think about some things—but they have some unexplained perceptions. Like the one that used to get sick if my wife Debie had a headache or cold and lay down during the day, even if she just stretched out on the divan.

When it comes to travel, dogs express their individuality. McGillicuddy howled. Michael McGillicuddy was called Mike most of the time, of course, but his full name added emphasis during crisis. He was a small Brittany without class and he belonged to Ben Williams. Dog handlers would have called him "soft" and non-professionals would have labeled him a canine sissy. He was not assertive or combative and felt the quickest way of settling a disagreement was to turn over on his back and roll his eyes pathetically. Blustering males who preferred to go through the whole domination procedure were disarmed by this ploy, and after standing over

McGillicuddy for a few seconds would begin to look foolish, and then slink away. But there was cunning.

McGillicuddy had a strong sense of fair play. When he felt that he was being mistreated he took what he considered the most urgent form of complaint. He howled. It was a big howl for so small a dog and it soared in a wolflike crescendo. It could be embarrassing. Like the time we camped with the little travel trailer in Washington State, where chukars lived on the banks of steep erosions with little rivers at their bottoms.

We'd been living in the little trailer in chukar country and felt the need for showers and a little civilization so we moved into a real trailer court for a few days. They parked us right near the entrance and just across from the washrooms—a place that seemed just a little too exposed for our outfit was looking pretty scroungy and most of the resident trailers looked permanent with flower boxes in their windows. We had two dogs, one of which was McGillicuddy, and although they slept inside the trailer at night we staked them outside during the day when they weren't hunting. It was only a short drive to chukars. Trouble began the first day.

I crossed the lane to the washroom and heard an eerie howl. Trailer occupants up and down the lane came out to see what was going on. The howler was McGillicuddy, who felt that when I left the trailer he was being abandoned to starvation or worse. During our stay at that park there was never any doubt when I went 50 yards to the washroom. We moved out to where there would be more privacy.

McGillicuddy's mild manners were deceiving and it took a long while for me to learn he was a troublemaker. Kelly, a brash, aggressive and larger Brittany type, who felt he should head up all dog operations, seemed to pick on McGillicuddy needlessly. After all, McGilly was always on the defensive, a fact which brought Kelly a few lumps. It was not unusual to be traveling on the highway with the two in the back of the old International Scout and to hear sounds of snarling rage, sounds indicating little McGillicuddy might be on the verge of being eaten. The logical procedure would be to stop and examine the situation. McGilly would invariably be on his back with Kelly standing over him, displaying fangs and growling ferociously. I would dress Kelly down and cuff him a little while McGilly registered grateful approval.

But I once happened to see the trouble start and from then on McGilly's whimpers of terror and Kelly's roars of rage brought little response. I happened to see the two lying in the truck when McGilly became bored. He reached over and swatted Kelly beside the head with his paw, a maneuver generally expected only from cats, small puppies and cartoon animals. Kelly came to life with an outraged snarl and was instantly standing over a prone and seemingly terrified McGilly. From then on such friction brought no human interference.

From time to time through this saga of dogs and birdshot there are other mentions of McGilly's unique traits and performances—accounts that indicate he was not exactly your typical bird dog. In fact, anyone who really understands gun dogs is likely to conclude that such timidity and such a retiring disposition are not likely to go with any usable bird pointer or retriever.

The fact is, however, that despite such impressions, Michael McGillicuddy was the best meat dog I ever followed, even though he pointed absent-mindedly and sometimes as if he were simply resting. He had a medium range and we followed him to pheasants, two kinds of quail, Huns, chukars, sharptailed grouse, sage hens and ruffed grouse. He could go all day, not really fast, but not plodding either, and was a persistent and successful dead hunter. His finding of cripples was spectacular and he understood exactly how the whole thing worked. He would creep behind you if you sneaked up to a spring creek with conversational mallards, knowing exactly what you were doing, and he took to water smoothly for ducks, or even geese. It was a goose that figured in another transportation item, a goose that caused old McGilly to lay down the law as to future operations. He resigned from goose retrieving.

I used to wonder if Ben let him in the water when it was too cold for Brittany fur but he lived to a very old age in good health. However, in his own way, he asserted himself concerning goose retrieving. Ben shot the Canada when there was some whispering slush ice slipping down a swift river and

McGilly swam to the bird out where the current curled and gurgled. He beached his goose almost a quarter mile downstream, meeting Ben who had scrambled along the bank through patches of brambles and across tangles of driftwood. That was when McGilly resigned. His teeth chattered.

Ben loaded McGilly and the goose into one of those older model Broncos. McGilly crowded to the far side of the little truck, plastered himself against the wall and refused to look at the goose on the other side. From then on, as far as I know, McGilly never gazed upon a goose, and when in a vehicle he kept as far away from one as he could. Rebellion. Passive resistance. Canine rights.

I thought McGillicuddy was too timid and too small to head up generations of bird hunters but I was wrong. He fathered a line of Brittanies that were a little bigger and a little bolder, and if they weren't quite so smart, they still had the go and the bird sense. It is kind of nice to see one of them as an orange and white spot on a ridgetop where I can squint my eyes a little and pretend that it's old McGilly with the Huns 30 feet ahead of his snub nose (he never crowded them).

I figured the other day that I hauled bird dogs for 9,000 miles over the main highways last year, indulging in a juvenile tendency to migrate with the bird seasons. After three or four years of that a dog begins to figure what's going on, and although he can't drive himself, he is beginning to think about it. I know dogs contemplate driving because we've had several that insisted on climbing into the driver's seat when we left the car to eat a cafe lunch. In a truck we have a barrier that discriminates against dogs. In the station wagon we let them ride on a specially constructed platform atop the luggage—built firm so they can nap in comfort. We soon learned that a soft and bouncy cushion isn't what a dog likes for long-term comfort.

The Duchess of Doonesbury, however, feels there is *some* discrimination involved in being kept out of the front seat. Since Dutch is big and sits tall, she creates something of a sensation when the car pulls in beside the cafe. She immediately hops into the front seat, always on the driver's side, managing the extreme gravity of a big square-jawed pointer with slightly long upper lips. She stares about as if watching traffic and stays there until we come out. Passing people think this is very funny but Dutch sees nothing unusual about it at all, feeling someone has to drive, even at the stops. Her long-term traveling companion, Spike the Brittany, seems to feel safe as long as Dutch is at the wheel. He rests calmly on the platform behind her.

I do not minimize the public relations impact of bird dogs but their effect varies with geography. In the South, passers-by at rest stops or motels will frequently study a pointer with great care, for pointers are quail dogs and the South is quail country. A Brittany is likely to be ignored except by friendly ladies who recognize a house pet when they see one. Once in a while someone will inquire as to "how that little setter lost his tail." Go to the West and the Brittany gets the atten-tion and Dutch is subjected to the ignominy of an inquiry as to "what kind of hound is that?"

This is not all just amusement for a migrant bird hunter. Take the example of Dutch in the central Texas parking lot. Now, as most quail hunters have learned, Texas isn't exactly wide open for tourists with shotguns. Texas quail country is pretty well sewed up by leases and by owners who are not entranced by strange hunters bombarding their quail. We were going through that country to a place where we knew we could hunt in a game management area and we knew we were presently in no-man's-land as far as casual gunning was concerned.

We stopped at the supermarket and Debie went in for something or other. I lowered the tailgate and the Duchess of Doonesbury stepped out on it for a breath of air, drawing herself up to her full 62 liver-and-white pounds and bestowing beatific smiles upon all who passed.

A lady passing with high-heeled boots, jeans and a shop-ping bag turned sharply in her course across the parking lot and came toward the truck.

"Is that big pointer as good as she looks?" she wanted to know.

I gave her my country boy, shoe-scuffing number and said ole Dutch did pretty well part of the time and found a few birds. The lady wanted to know if we were going hunting and I said we were heading farther south, that I figured the country near the supermarket was pretty well sewed up.

"It sure is," the lady said, displaying a bond of understanding with Dutch, who cocked her head a little and waited for further comment. "But I've got a ranch out here with a hell-slather lot of bobwhites. You bring that big pointer out there and we'll blow the stew out of them!"

It was a rather indelicate invitation for gentleman's sport but after that I eyed Dutch in the rearview mirror with new respect.

If you travel far in a truck or car, your dogs quickly learn about rest stops. They learn to hit the ground, run hard and be ready to load up again in five minutes. They may snooze until the turn signal clicks on or the tires hit gravel, but when one of those things happens they are likely to be instantly and whiningly ready for recreation. They are a little disgusted by interstate highway rest stops where there's a sign that all pets must be kept on a leash.

Confident that no reader will send the state police after me, I confess that I don't always observe those rules when there are few people at a rest stop, which is generally the case during fall hunting season. Likely as not, there's a grassy or even weedy area back of the picnic tables and restrooms and when I get the dogs back there I unsnap the leads and let them run for a little piece. They know the whole story, are aware of the rules, and seldom wander very far. Works fine.

In North Dakota there were quite a few people at the rest stop but it was mid-September and I saw no state employees. Didn't walk quite as far from the car as usual before I unsnapped the leads and the two pointers scratched off toward the fence 50 yards away—but they didn't go far. They froze in rigid points to the edification of all and sundry present, right there by the leash sign. A furtive whistle toot had no effect and I did the only thing I could do. I walked past them and cringed when a blizzard of Hungarian partridges swarmed out and about to the cheers of onlookers. The dogs were disappointed that we didn't shoot or follow singles. They were a little hard to corral and I was relieved to close the tailgate on their slavering countenances. I am not sure of the penalty for such trespasses but I have been more careful since. There was another time when a cock pheasant had taken up residence by the rest stop fence and neither whistle nor hissed imprecations would stay my dogs from their stealthy search and rigid points. And speaking of pheasants. . .

Superior, Wisconsin is a nice town and the Holiday Inn looked very good to us as we trucked westward from Michigan where I had botched a job on woodcock. It was night and it was raining, a chill fall rain that pinched visibility and wiggled the neon lights.

"Where'll we run the dogs?" Debie wondered in the perpetual inquiry of our travels.

"Looks like a weed patch over there," I said, peering through the dripping truck window at a vague outline well away from the motel across the parking lot and farther. So, while Debie set up housekeeping with the overnight luggage I led Dutch the pointer and Spike the Brittany off toward the rain-blurred exercise spot. It began to rain harder but I had a rain jacket and some hunting boots. I turned them loose at the grass and weed patch, which seemed bigger than it had looked from the motel entrance. The stuff was higher too.

The dogs hit the wall of weeds and disappeared. I couldn't make them out back in there, they didn't seem to be bouncing and I had forgotten the damned flashlight. I called and nothing appeared. I blew the whistle until my ears rang and heard nothing in return except the steadily rising mutter of rain. The wind was up a little. I made some remarks about the dogs and walked into the wet weeds. I stepped into a ditch full of water. I said some more things about dogs and stumbled into a vestpocket marsh. Dryness was a forgotten objective.

I came upon a wet, spotted blob of something which, it turned out, was Spike. He was pointing. I grabbed him and snapped a lead to his collar in violation of all training rules and dragged him behind me. A little farther on a cock pheasant cackled up under my feet and blew off through the darkness toward Lake Superior. Spike considered this a very sloppy handling performance and evidently didn't know whether to point the flying bird or bite me.

It was a little later that I found Dutch, also pointing, but when her pheasant left she tried to avoid the lead. I tackled her and dragged both of them toward the Holiday Inn sign, which flickered through sheets of rain. You can get only so wet, I philosophised. I fell into a ditch again. One dog was pulling ahead and the other was holding back in preparation for jumping it.

In the Holiday Inn room it was cozy with the odor of wet dogs and wet clothing. After a hot shower I slept pretty well but at intervals during the night I thought I heard strange sounds from where the dogs were penned. I could have sworn they were giggling.

Penned? Well, yes. We learned early in the game that a dog needs his own spot in a motel. Otherwise, he might walk across the bed or peer through the curtains and bark at passing motel managers. We don't let them sleep on the carpets. We have a tarpaulin we put down for them. We trained one dog to stay on a towel with "Miami Beach" inscribed in big letters. He grew up on it and grew old with it, and when he was through with it, it was pretty ragged but he had known it was for sleeping and he never chewed it. However, as time went on it became a game to see how far he could lead off and still touch it, like a jittery first-base runner. The fence is better.

The "fence" is only a foot or so high and it is plastic coated wire that doesn't scratch—the kind of stuff used for small flower beds. We put it down as soon as we move in and enclose the dogs with it, keeping them against a wall. They learn fast. Put them behind it and tell them to stay. When one hops or steps over it we simply pick him up and toss him gently back where he came from. Stay! They learn in an evening or two and run for the pen as soon as they enter the room. The pen with its tarp and no-spill water container is security.

We lost old Kelly once in a little back-country motel. We were pheasant hunting and three of us were moving in our duffel when we first missed him. When we finally found him he was in the back of the clothes closet. Two years before we'd stayed at the same place and put his bed in there.

Now there are some motels that do not take kindly to dogs, their managers relating horror stories of pets that dismantled rooms, had digestive problems on expensive carpets, barked all night or threatened guests. These discriminatory hostleries are most frequently found in hunting country and the reason is plain if you'll stop and think.

Most cross-country tourists who take their dogs with them are used to it and their dogs behave themselves as experienced travelers. But in good bird country it's not unusual for a party to arrive with dogs and guns, the dogs fresh from the kennel and never having traveled before—or at least not since last hunting season. Such visitors can make all dogs unwelcome.

Dogs that spend the night in the truck or wagon can sometimes become overly protective and be pretty noisy about people walking past. The "No Pets" sign is accepted as one of the tribulations of dog travel unless it is raining and a long way to the next motel. Then it becomes a personal insult. Even if there isn't a "No Pets" sign I would rather not have to walk past the registration desk with dogs. Dutch, the 62-pound pointer, looks more and more like a pony as I approach the desk, and if she comes up with a baritone woof or two of greeting for the clerk I try to look smaller, and feel that way.

Debie walked up to the desk. It was raining and a long way to someplace else in Kansas. There was a "No Pets" sign.

"Oops," said Debie, "I guess you don't want any part of us and our dogs."

She turned and headed for the door.

"Aw, that's a sign the boss put up," said the girl behind the desk. "He doesn't like dogs. I like dogs. Bring 'em in!"

We had one dog who considered a cross-country trip a perfect way to survey a few thousand miles of hunting country. He wanted his window opened so he could keep a nose out there to catch whiffs of quail in Missouri, prairie chickens in Kansas, pheasants in Iowa. It was quite a charge to watch him light up as we passed birdy-looking hedges or draws. We didn't know at that time that too much high-speed snuffing was a little hard on a dog's olfactory mechanism and that he'd be better off with less scenting. A veterinarian explained it. And once a party of tourists honked and flagged us down. They were wide-eyed and well-meaning.

"Your dog has his nose caught in a window crack!" they screamed.

The reading of passing scents, even with the windows closed, goes on constantly. For years we have hunted each season in sagebrush country and with their first breath of sage after months away from it our dogs get excited. One used to become ill every time he smelled it for the first time in the fall. Car sick? Nope. Sage happy.

Then we come to the South from snow and grouse and the dogs gradually become more and more interested in the odors of quail country—palmetto, pines, wire grass, broom sedge and oaks. And they recognize the smells of home from some distance away, even if they arrive in the night and have been away for months.

There are dogs that whine and whimper when they think they are going hunting and now and then one will bark or give so ear-piercing a squeal that harsh measures are called for.

You leave the house and they patter around in their compartment in the truck. On the freeway they yawn and nap. At the rest stops they bounce and pretend they are trying to break out.

Then you leave a highway and the truck tires find a rutted road or noisy gravel. The rig lurches and bounces and the dogs become conversational within seconds. They know it's hunting country and I guess I can put up with their racket.

If definition of game bird scents is instinct, choice of the right ones is acquired. There is the quail specialist which refuses to point woodcock at first, although they say he can nearly always be converted to timberdoodle odors. Some refuse forever to retrieve woodcock, obviously because of a scent they don't like. To me, woodcock smells much like a duck, but I have no registration papers.

Chapter Three

False Points, Blind Retrieves and Other Mysteries

If a solid point is the only dog work he recognizes, a hunter has missed much pleasure and probably has trudged past many birds. The thoughtful man behind a bird dog gets his shots through a process he can never fully understand, but he learns to read the signs.

The expert dog handler who details the mysteries of scent speaks from as crude an olfactory system as that of his pupils, and the hunting dog's nose is so many times more sensitive than a human's that our personal experience with odors is almost worthless.

Perhaps a smoking object laid on the ground comes nearest to a visual demonstration of the routes of game bird scent. It may go swiftly with the wind close to the earth, it may rise slowly into still air, and it may spread and cling to the ground. But always it becomes less dense with its distance from the source, and that source may not be obvious on some days. And where the smoke has passed, we cannot see the residue that clings to earth, plant and stone.

Dog noses vary in sensitivity, but only occasionally is there a blooded hunter with so poor a nose that he hunts badly. More often his deficiencies are in adaptability and under-standing.

There was Lola (I shall not defame her breed) who was that occasional exception, her dull nose accompanied by slovenly and thoughtless hunting habits. Occasionally she backed other dogs, but more frequently she loped into a covey of birds and then cowered in horror at their explosion. Her owner, who kept her for vague family reasons, finally stopped punishing her for that. Lola, he said, couldn't smell her own dish and was as surprised as anyone else when she stumbled upon game. But one day during a pheasant hunt, Lola froze in a small patch of woods and no other dog was near. "That bird," said her owner, "will be within a foot of her nose."

It was, and after he shot it he added, "Lola can't smell as well as I can, and when she points you'd better believe!" And I was pressed by the nagging thought that a dog with a hypersensitive nose might well be a false pointer and become over-cautious.

There are days when scenting conditions are poor: hot, dry days when scent disappears or never forms, rainy days when it is washed away, and cold days when the birds move little and seem to release none of it at all. But there are days like none of these when good dogs seem noseless and the old theories wear thin.

There was the quail that fell end-over-end with a little trail of feathers to land somewhere beyond the Florida palmettos, and when two veteran pointers and a pup went after it, they could find nothing in an amphitheater of short grass. After they had given up, my friend happened to see the dead bird, breast up, and called the pup for training purposes. The puppy stood over the dead bird (he hadn't touched it) and looked confused. Then my friend called his best pointer, told her to hunt dead, and finally gave up when she stood and looked at him with her foot an inch from the quail. The next bird we killed fell in somewhat denser cover and was never found at all. A day when dead birds gave no scent?

We flew a covey that scattered, and only I was watching the single that I shot 30 yards away over a little hillside. I kept my eyes on the exact spot; this one I would find myself. But when the pointer that had failed so miserably before was told to hunt dead, she went head-high straight to my kill and retrieved it, apparently catching the scent from a full 50 feet. That bird gave off scent. Similar events are common, although generally less dramatic, and the theory that some dead birds, or even live ones, can actually produce no scent at all is hard to refute, regardless of unscientific status.

Gunners who have become blasé about the acuity of dog noses still marvel at their selectivity, and no discussion of hunting dogs goes long without a story of one that has stopped its retrieve of a dead bird to point a live one, detecting the scent of a living quarry several feet away with a dead one an inch from its nostrils. Remarkable? Not as remarkable as the retrieving dog that scents another *dead* bird on its way in, for what is the difference in the scent of those two dead birds that fell a split second apart? Or is it some finely-drawn discernment of the direction from which a thread of scent has come? And what if the dog has been sprayed by a cranky skunk an hour earlier?

A man can sit in his living room and tell you he smells nothing at all; at least he is conscious of no odors. Give him a whiff of frying ham, and he thinks he smells that and nothing else. So if his nose is selective, it is crudely so, and he records nothing but the exceptional odors. But visually he is highly selective, and he'll find a small object of interest in a vast scene containing a thousand larger things. The dog's nose is as selective as the man's eyes.

Does a single quail five feet away smell as strongly as a dozen 20 feet away, and does the experienced dog know the difference? I say he does.

There were the two Brittanies, veteran Hungarian partridge campaigners, and when careful, meticulous old Mike pointed on the ridgetop, high-headed, covey-hunting Hogan came in carefully and backed him briefly, then back-pedaled for several feet and began a cautious quartering, farther and farther away to my embarrassment. When we walked in on Mike's point, a single bird whirred down the canyon, but Hogan hadn't been satisfied with the scent of only one Hun. He'd thought the main covey must be nearby, and it was. Such snobbish activities would not be field trial triumphs.

There are those who boast of cold-nosed wizards who can work into a covey from afar, going birdy for long distances before a point is made, and there is no question that bird scent can carry a quarter-mile in ideal conditions. But often the work is on running birds, and the dog is following them rather than catching long-range shreds of their odor. The veteran dog reader usually knows. Generally speaking, sustained birdiness and constant movement mean birds a long way off, while the running ones are indicated by a series of brief points and stealthy moves. Running birds can be the undoing of dogs trained on tightly-holding game, and they require some special canine logic.

How does the scent path reveal moving birds rather than vagaries of the wind? I do not know, but it does.

The setter quarters fast and high-headed through wavy western prairie grass and turns suddenly in a half-point, only to continue his cast. A mistake? A lark or sparrow? Note the spot where he paused. A minute later, on another swing, he breaks stride again, and the watching hunter sees that it is on the same stream of air, even though far from the original signal. A pattern is emerging, even though it may be several passes later when the dog abandons his methodical grid and goes definitely birdy to point or quarter tightly toward the sharptails. A thousand dogs have been whistled away from such birds by owners who recognize only solid points.

The smoke-hued shorthair goes slow in the brown weeds of autumn, now an infantryman instead of a lancer, his nostrils expanded with the scent story of the moving ringneck ahead. The dog's head is low most of the time, but lifted occasionally for a different stratum of the scent; the watchful hunter hurries behind, ready for the wild flush. And then the scent relates that the bird has stopped, as it has stopped briefly several times before, but this time the old dog, pointing firmly, sees the gleaming gun barrel beside him. Now is the time, and before the bird can decide to run again, the dog leaps, not at the unseen bird but straight up to come back down in his own tracks. And the sudden movement changes the slinking cock into slapping wings and excited cackles.

The pointer gives up too soon, the angry gunner thinks, and the hard-hit chukar is still unfound. Repeatedly the dog moves off, obviously to hunt for more birds, and he is irritably called back to the scene until even his disgusted employer gives up. Then, after the hunter has walked hundreds of yards and has momentarily lost track of his dog, the pointer comes at a run from an unsuspected arroyo, the lost chukar in his mouth. The remorseful gunner can no more apologize than the dog can explain how the trail led farther than an obtuse human could have expected.

Chukar hunters frequently endure false points at the edges of hazy canyons, but they soon learn that air currents from the depths may rise or fall in baffling eddies. And while such swirls of provocative scents can make distances deceptive even for expert dogs, there are other cases when the solid scent of nearby game can completely disappear without a true flush.

To the chagrin of the faithful, ruffed grouse have somewhat different habits in various parts of the country, the roaring flush giving way to crafty schemes. Along one willowed brook I know, there is a scatter of spruce, thick trees that could hide a bird forever. Along that brushy watercourse, I can follow my dog only by his bell, and when the tinkling stops I begin a stumbling, thrashing charge to where I think it was last heard. But all too often, the cessation of the tinkle is followed quickly by a brief whir of wings. The bird has simply gone straight up into a spruce, and when I reach the dog he stands stupidly on an unproductive and unsteady point or stares blankly upward. His nose will no longer help me, for the bird and its scent are generally above our heads.

One old thinker abandoned scenting efforts at such times, and when I arrived he would look into the tree and bark. Field trial purists please note.

Only a beginning hunter is surprised when, after being out of sight for a time his dog invariably appears from the rear in the simple, early-acquired expedient of cutting his master's trail through a single wide circle. Late on a warm Florida day, ending a hunt the easy way by walking homeward on an abandoned asphalt road, I missed my Brittany. I stopped and waited, strongly doubting he could be on a point in that particular area. Then, far behind me, I saw a white speck, not coming toward me but going in and out of the thick brush at the point I'd stepped on the pavement with rubber-soled pacs. He simply couldn't trail me on that road, and when I went back far enough to call him, he came at top speed. Minutes later, he was lost again, and I finally held him at heel for the remaining mile of pavement.

Hound men are often frustrated when the quarry runs on plowed ground or "hard roads," and although odor can rise through water or hang to its surface, a moving stream can take the fox's scent with it.

Interpretation of hot trails is less complex, but no one has explained how a hound follows cold scent without backtracking half of the time. Is it that the scent clings most strongly to the side of objects opposite the quarry's direction?

Through breeding we have bent scenting instinct to our hunting uses, and perhaps we have honed it through selection, although some breeds may simply ignore the essential hunting odors because they have had no need of them. No human can realize the impact of strong quail scent upon a pointer's nostrils or mallard scent on a Labrador's.

The composed and confident Brittany puppy was to be a good dog one day, but I had lacked time and had neglected his field trips, so he was several months old without a contact with the birds he was bred to hunt. Near the end of bird season, Buddy Nordmann came by, fresh from a hunt, and took a single dead quail from his coat. "Let's see what your pup thinks of it," he said, and he offered the bobwhite. The response was not exactly what I expected.

The pup's eyes bulged wildly as he accepted the bird, his entire body shook pathetically, and he drooled furiously, his rasping breath turning the saliva to streams of froth. He looked furtively about with no attention to us. Then he laid the quail reverently on the ground—and threw up. "That pup is pretty birdy," Buddy said.

The pup wasn't exactly selective, and if there were conflicting human and hunting-coat odors on the quail, he probably never noticed them. But anyone who has worked dogs on planted birds knows there are some fine hunters who will ignore those that have been handled. Two of us once tried planted quail on three dogs at once. One pointed, another backed, and the third, a big mature pointer, looked disgusted and walked away. We tried it with the scorner alone, and he hunted briefly, found the plant and turned his back on it. We knew when we were whipped.

Of course it must have been the human scent on the planted quail, but remember that there was human scent everywhere, which is true in many game fields. So how does a dog know what human scent comes from the quail and what comes from a hunter approaching downwind?

If definition of game bird scents is instinct, choice of the right ones is acquired. There is the quail specialist which refuses to point woodcock at first, although they say he can nearly always be converted to timberdoodle odors. Some refuse forever to retrieve woodcock, obviously because of a scent they don't like. To me, woodcock smells much like a duck, but I have no registration papers.

Ben Williams uses a Brittany as a retriever while jump-shooting mallards on a Montana creek and marsh. The little guy seems to enjoy waterfowl (although he swore off Canada geese at the edge of an icy river some years back), and he sticks close at heel on such expeditions, although a fairly wide ranger on upland hunts. Undoubtedly he sometimes receives pheasant scent in the little creek bottom, but he had always remained faithful to the primary objective—until the day Ben shot the snipe.

The duck hunting was over that evening, and we were carrying some birds toward our car when the snipe flushed. Ben automatically felled it with a duck load. The little Brittany found and retrieved it, then abandoned his passive role at heel, began quartering the marsh and pointing snipe. I don't know how many seasons he had walked past them on the way to the creek, but when he thought we wanted them, he had no difficulty in sorting out their scent, long catalogued but never attended.

It is elementary to work pointing dogs upwind when possible, but when the hunt must go with the wind, the thoughtful hunter will encourage longer casts so the dog will have more room to handle game between him and the gun, a simple ruse often ignored. More regrettably, the wise old campaigner, driving his extra-deep swath in order to face a bit of breeze, is sometimes pulled in emphatically by a creature who hasn't the slightest idea of what birds smell like upwind or downwind.

No upland hunter can alter a dog's scenting ability or really know its thoughts, but there are times when he can use superior vision to direct a superior nose—when a pointing or a flushing dog working game stops in confusion at a wind-scrubbed stony area, or when a woodcock weaves a confused scent pattern while pattering about inside a thicket. If the hunter knows cover he may have helpful ideas, and if he studies his dog he learns when it is confused.

But it is equally important that he recognize the dog's department and that he not confuse canine cogitation with stupidity. Indecision is not always ineptitude, and there are quail hunters who can note almost instantly that their pointers are being sidetracked by "stinkbirds." And although a dog is trained not to point rabbits, perhaps he cannot ignore one completely.

"He doesn't have birds up there," a seasoned Hun hunter told me when I began to scramble up a rocky slope toward a dog obviously working game. "That's a rabbit. See how his tail points down. See how guilty he looks. See how he swipes a quick look at me." Of such things are dog-hunter relationships made through the seasons.

"Come on, Jerry!" the hunter yelled, "You're no beagle. Let's find some birds!" And the dog, caught at his private bunny search, put up his head and resumed Hun hunting.

And the quail dog changes his classic stance a little. His head moves. "He's got them," the owner states, "But they've moved and scattered and he doesn't know where they are. Watch it because you may kick one up any time."

Such interpretations smack of the occult to those who feel only that a point is a point and a pointer simply hunts until he freezes.

There on the street in early morning you smell frying ham—or is it bacon? And just where does it come from? It really isn't very important because you don't make your living sorting smells. And your own little catalog of odors is a sort of scent primer, of strong smells in large mental letters, with no space for the thousands of odors you do not record at all.

We don't shoot the camphor tree birds any more because there's a church just a little way from where they live and there are some new houses too. The joggers go by on the road just a hundred yards away, but the quail are still there. In spring, I drive down the lane beside the trees and hear the lovelorn cock birds yelling their name as if life depended on it. Perhaps it does.

Chapter Four

Buddies, and Others

Not many tourists would have timed the little flock of ring-bills hissing in to a roadside canal, passing us on the Florida Turnpike as if we were having car trouble.

"Let's see," Buddy Nordmann said. "We're going fifty-five and they have to be doing sixty-some and they're already killing their speed to land. Did you ever try to figure the lead on one of those little varmints when he's power-diving over a lake? He sounds like a five-inch shell."

A newspaper feature writer once said it doesn't take long to get tired of white birds and spindly trees and that, all in all, there is too much of Florida's Turnpike. It may be that Northerners hurrying to gleaming hotels and beaches have little interest in weedy creeks and palmetto flats broken by little clumps of pines. Certainly a single alligator dozing among the rushes in a barrow pit, if noticed at all, can't compete with hundreds of them lolling on artificial islands under an "Alligator Farm" sign. And humped Brahman cattle with their attendant cattle egrets become tiresome if you're heading for Sea World and its trained killer whale.

Buddy Nordmann and I were hunting quail. "This country right along here," he said, "won't support very many birds but there should be a bunch living at the edge of that oak hammock over there. Everything they need with water along that little creek and some thick stuff to hide in if things get rough." Thinking like a quail comes naturally to people like Nordmann. Part of the time at least, hunting and gunning are two different things. And although *gunning* sounds a bit more cultured, somebody must find the birds first. Growing up with a few coveys of quail is a help. Bunches like the camphor tree covey.

The row of camphors, almost stately now, has had those birds since the trees were little more than bushes and for years Nordmann and his friends worked the camphor covey with succeeding generations of pointers. Nordmann began his quail shooting with an old hammer double when his hands were small.

"Both hammers come back pretty fast when you get used to it," he said.

Twice I helped pursue the camphor covey, traveling there in style on Manon Halcomb's Jeep with a high seat and with three lean and anxious pointers in the dog box—a wide-goer with an electric beeper, a medium dog you could see most of the time and a close-in expert who seldom got more than 75 yards out. But we always left plenty for seed. In fact, after the first visit of the season the birds might take care of that.

We don't shoot the camphor tree birds any more because there's a church just a little way from where they live and there are some new houses too. The joggers go by on the road just a hundred yards away, but the quail are still there. In spring, I drive down the lane beside the trees and hear the lovelorn cock birds yelling their name as if life depended on it. Perhaps it does.

In a good year there will be several coveys near the camphors, over in the weeds by the pines and down among the oaks or in the unused field near the church where they had to use a bush hog last year. When the rain comes at the wrong time or there are too many cotton rats there may be only the one small covey, but that succession has lasted for 40 years.

These Florida towns grow outward through the pines and oaks and across the old orange groves and many a brushpatch hunter has found a split-level house where he meant to put down his dog. The brushpatcher is a vanishing breed and few pointers sleep on Florida porches any more, largely replaced here by decorative poodles; bird hunting is serious business now, carried on by kennel residents for gunners who own or lease bird land. A few birds on the edge of town after work is almost a thing of the past. The quail may still be there but they are on the edges of golf courses or backyards.

"I'll tell you where to find a few birds," Nordmann said when I wanted some dog exercise that wouldn't take but a couple of hours. "Go out there by the county dump and back past the chicken farm and there's a weed patch. Everybody hunts it but at the wrong time. Get there just before sunset. They come out of the timber then."

The pattern is old for hard-hunted country and it gives rise to the terms "swamp quail" and "one-shot coveys." Such birds do their feeding in only a few minutes and no more than a few yards from dense cover. They go back with the sound of voices or the mutter of a hunting-truck's engine, and otherwise efficient dogs snuffle helplessly at the swamp's edge.

Buddy's little weed field was crisscrossed with the wide-treaded tracks of hunting rigs that had made brief passes there before going to bigger country. It was one of those times every hunter has known when things are not right, when he feels he is wasting his time and when his dog stares inquiries at him. I could hear the chicken farm and a distant din of barking meant feeding time at the animal shelter in the other direction. I wondered who owned the little field. There was no fence or sign; brush and oaks marked the edges.

My Brittany, used to foolish quests in strange cover, made a point almost against a wall of brush backed by live oaks and I suspected meadow larks or rabbits. But I walked over there and the quail buzzed up the way swamp quail do, not in a compact group but already scattering to find individual gaps in the forest. I poked the little double at one bird and missed—probably a good thing since at that range there would have been little to retrieve. On the second shot I was more composed and my bird brushed through a bush as it fell, leaving three or four feathers on the thorns. George Bird Evans says yokel writers always tell of missing the first shot and hitting with the second but, by golly, that's the way it was.

After that the chicken farm cackled again and dogs at the animal shelter loudly requested a second helping. A heavy truck went by on the road behind me. It was not exactly the kind of sylvan retreat preferred by Thoreau but there was a second covey a little farther along. The sun was down and bullbats appeared as I went to the car.

"There should have been another bunch in there somewhere," Buddy said the next day. "They've been there since I was a kid."

But then, Buddy Nordmann is the fellow who called a wild bobwhite rooster out of the palmettos and finally had it perched on his boot toe, still looking for the origin of the seductive feminine whistles Buddy was producing. Nordmann is a fellow who follows swamp quail into the swamp with a Labrador retriever and a riot gun. I mention this last because quail are also hunted from rubber-tired wagons with matched mules and long-eared pointers that are almost airborne. Buddy's swamp penetration is hardly traditional but if it is unfair it is unfair to the gunner. For that matter I find it difficult to scorn grouse hunters who use pistols and take only head shots.

Buddy Pigg of Tennessee is in the men's clothing business. He dresses impeccably, drives impeccable cars and runs impeccable setters and pointers. He is suave and educated in a politely relaxed way and the last man to be accused of superstition but his shooting vest is tattered and occasionally dirty. I would not suggest that it contributes to his marksmanship but gunning psychology is a misty field I shall not transgress.

I noticed Buddy Pigg's quail gun right away. (I am sorry that we deal here with two *Buddys* but perhaps the nickname *is* somehow associated with bobwhites.) I recognized Buddy Pigg's gun instantly for the same design as Frank Woolner's grouse model. It was a Model 59 Winchester, glass-barreled and pared down by master gunsmithing until there was little to swing but some fine checkering.

He very seldom misses quail. I am tired of reading descriptions of gunning perfection but I have noted that it is often approached by quail specialists. Evidently a good shot can *learn* quail flight patterns, perhaps subconsciously, until his percentage is unusual. I believe the fine quail shot is more consistent than the fine dove shot, or even the fine duck shot.

Buddy Pigg also refuses to shoot at a clay target and when I met him at a Mississippi shooting plantation he turned away from a party of gunners pecking away at a practice range.

"That fellow's going to mess himself up," he commented as a shooter inked a wide right angle. I was chagrined because I had hoped to shoot a few clays to demonstrate I am not as bad a shot as I had appeared on bobwhites earlier that day.

But there are plenty of good shots and we are discussing quail *hunting.*

These were wild quail we were after but they had been attracted to feed plots and a big covey went up far out and spread as it sailed over a low oak ridge and went into a brushy hollow. We followed and the dogs seemed to have suffered a complete loss of nose.

"They'll be right over here," Buddy said. "We'll just walk them up."

A bird flushed at his feet and fell at the measured distance that marks the businesslike quail gunner. Another did the same. I clutched sweatily at my gun but kicked out no birds at all. Buddy shot some more singles and decided we'd worked over that covey enough.

At first I thought I was just unlucky but it dawned on me that there was something else going on. I fished humbly for an explanation and Pigg finally confessed with obvious embarrassment that he guessed he knew where individual birds would be sitting. I had been picking out areas with cover that was too dense. First, Pigg finally said, you must remember that a bird wants more room to fly than I had thought—and it is careful to put something between it and the place it originally flushed from. So I turned and stared back at the little hollow and saw I had been where the cover was too thick, just a little, and Pigg had been walking where it was a little thicker than the thinnest, but not as thick as the thickest—Ah, the hell with it!

When a species ranges nearly from coast to coast and feeds upon a list of things that fills pages of a quail text, it is certain to be hunted in a variety of ways. Palmetto quail have special qualifications requiring bird dogs with specific talents.

Forrest Ware clucks to his setter when he needs help in getting a bird to fly, a procedure that takes both human and canine judgment. Pointers who turn into flush dogs when they enter the dark wilderness of the palmetto patch require gunners attuned to the system. And they need bells sometimes, bells that will scare hard-hunted birds in the open.

The birds will hardly ever be in the patch to begin with but after the flush you see the covey fan out and balance delicately on their stubby set of wings to disappear in the palmettos, appearing impenetrable to a stranger. The ground under the palmettos is darkened from the thick fronds but there is some room down there for a bird to scuttle.

Feeling like an imbecile and watching for rattlesnakes, I once crawled into a heavy palmetto patch on hands and knees to see what a dog sees. It isn't much and it is no wonder a pointer looks surprised when he finally comes out in the open. He's probably never where he thought he would be unless he backtrailed himself.

Forrest Ware has been a professional dog trainer and when I watch him standing up to his elbows in brush or palmettos and staring warily about to find where the dog is I am a little disappointed with him—for his instructions are cryptic and efficient and lack the color of those used by a long-gone friend of mine who could have inspired a crippled football team or a pinned-down rifle squad.

There in the thick he would eye the slight movements of the palmetto tops that marked his dog's questing route in the depths. The instructions were musical and borrowed from speech of the Deep South—dialect saved for scared pointers snuffing in the half light. It went:

"*Dat* bird a-runnin! Hunt'im *close* in dere—*close* in dere!"

Sing it and repeat it and when a bobwhite roars up through the palmettos, boosted by a dog's nose, he'll sound like a dozen. It is only one more way to hunt quail.

They say a man is entitled to one good hunting dog in a lifetime. I guess I've had mine.

Chapter Five

Kelly, He Got Them All

When we buried old Kelly we put up a plaque with the names of 18 upland birds burned into it. He'd pointed all of them from Alaska to Mexico and I wrote a book about them.

To this day nobody else has come forth to announce that his dog has pointed all 18 major species of North American game birds so I guess it's more unusual than I thought at the time. There may be some who figure the list could be broken down further and some who think we overdid it but our figure comes to 18 kinds of birds, and I've heard no complaints.

Now Kelly was a Brittany, a breed that comes on pretty slowly in the South where "bird dogs" are pointers with palmetto scratches on their ears. A Brittany is a spaniel that points like a setter. Kelly weighed about 38 pounds, was orange and white, fairly long-haired, and had a bobbed tail like other Brittanies. A male pointer will weigh 50 pounds or more in most cases and I have heard Kelly called a "little fuzzy dog." There is a lady who owns a quail plantation up near Monticello, is world famous for her fine pointers, and who calls Brittanies "snuffle pups." But she keeps a few of them around the place.

Frank Woolner, a famous gunner and author, is like some other bird hunters who feel a bird dog should have a long tail. Woolner wrote me that Brittanies work fine but he never could get used to shooting grouse over an Easter bunny. Kelly couldn't have cared less about such comments, figuring a pocket bird dog gets to make more trips, lives comfortably in a one-man mountain tent (with the man) and slides into a motel without attracting too much attention. Any canine who does all those things is likely to have personality and ideas of his own. Kelly did.

Take retrieving. Kelly would bring the bird if you couldn't get to it yourself but he reasoned that he didn't have hands and it was an imposition to expect him to carry things around when it was easier for you. Shoot a bobwhite in short grass and he wouldn't touch it but when I spilled a ptarmigan over an Alaska cliff he clattered down after it, down into the mists hell-bent, just hitting the rocks now and then. I never expected him to get back but he did, and he had the bird, clawing his way over the edge again. When he knew I could see it he threw it down and went hunting.

When he was a pup we took him with us to work on some planted, penraised quail along with some young pointers. That's when he pointed his first quail and was doing such a good job of it that the preserve operator, wearing polished boots, told me I should walk up, pat him and tell him he was a good dog. I did, although I was apprehensive. Kelly immediately lay down to have his belly scratched, to the amazement of a rigid pointer who was backing him. After getting the recognition he felt he deserved, Kelly wriggled happily, sniffed the grass and flowers with appreciation, then arose and again snapped into a classy point. The quail was surprised too, I think. I could see him plainly three feet away.

I don't shoot very well and Kelly was quite tolerant of me but he knew Buddy Nordmann was with it. After he gained experience he could make a federal case of pointing a single quail. He'd go though an elaborate stalking procedure, looking back at you as if to say, "Man, he's here and you'd better be ready!"

By the time Kelly actually pointed, many shooters would be a little unstrung. He did the whole bit for Buddy who doesn't miss very much. On this one occasion Buddy missed—twice. Kelly watched the quail disappear into the old orange grove and then looked sorrowfully toward Buddy who was standing there in shock. Kelly's heart brimmed with compassion. He trotted back to Buddy, put his paws on Buddy's belt and looked sympathetically up into Buddy's red face.

Buddy reacted.

"Call off your damn dog!" he said.

Kelly charged hard when he hunted. That's how he broke his front leg and that's why he'd get overheated on warm Florida days. He'd take frequent breaks, digging holes to cool off in, and places where he'd hunted frequently looked like old battlefields.

A quail went up high to clear some trees and I miraculously nailed it so that it plunged into an area where I couldn't mark it down. Kelly went in to look for it but he didn't come back and after a little whistling and yelling I went in to look for him. I finally found him flattened out on his stomach in a fresh hole. He looked up when I came floundering through the brush and I made some remarks about his goofing off when there was a bird down. He reached over to where the bird was lying beside him and flipped the quail toward me with his nose.

Case closed.

He then cooled off for three or four minutes before going back to work.

He had a sense of humor. In his youth he continually ran afoul of skunks. He didn't hurt them, just managed to fool around until they doused him. There was once when my wife greeted me with a jug of vinegar as I dismounted from the truck.

"I smelled you when you turned in the driveway," she said. Kelly strolled over to get his bath.

Then Kelly decided skunks were a joke and he didn't get too close to them any more. There was the time when he pointed at the wreckage of an old wagon and I went over and kicked it. No doubt then as to what was hiding under the wagon and as I whirled about to escape I saw that Kelly was already 50 yards away where he had headed as I aimed the kick. He was grinning happily.

In some of the country we hunted there were quite a few porcupines. Some dogs repeatedly get quilled and I can de-quill a dog blindfolded although it can be pretty tough on the dog. As far as I know Kelly never in all his life got a single quill in him.

Kelly always scorned Murphy, a big square-headed English pointer I used to hunt Hungarian partridge. Murphy wasn't much of a thinker and Kelly considered him a congenital idiot. He loved to see Murphy in trouble.

Murphy pointed at the edge of some brush and Kelly backed him gleefully and kept turning and looking at me as I hurried up from 200 yards away.

I couldn't hear him but I am sure Kelly said, "Boss, you gotta' see this. Come on."

Then while I was still 50 yards away, Kelly tippy-toed up beside Murphy who was all charged up and quivering anyway.

"Yip!" said Kelly right in Murphy's ear, and Murphy charged.

Poor old Murphy landed right on a big, irritated porky and gave a pathetic howl of pain. Kelly disappeared and it was only when I got out the pliers and took a death grip on Murph that he came back to watch me pull the quills. It made his whole day and he grinned ecstatically.

As he grew older Kelly learned his combat limitations but he had definite opinions of other dogs. He was peaceful most of the time but there were certain dogs he didn't like and never would. One of these was Iron Mike, a larger Brittany who had spent his youth in the street and knew his way around. Mike was too big to fit the Brittany specifications and I think a setter got under a fence somewhere in his ancestry, even though he was properly registered.

The feud really started when I somehow picked up Kelly after picking up Iron Mike from a friend's kennel. This was an insult. That was Kelly's truck. In somebody else's car he was the polite guest. To be greeted by a big ugly dog already in his own vehicle was too much, and on the way to the hunting grounds Kelly kept growling at a pitch seemingly far too low for so small a dog. He sounded a little like a stuck Jeep. Mike, who was not used to being pushed around, growled back.

They worked together all day but just before going in we put them down to hunt one more spot and apparently we put them out of the truck too close together. Maybe I set one of them on top of the other as I unloaded. Anyway, they turned into a blurred ball of brindle fur from which came sounds like feeding time at the zoo.

I am not too good at breaking up dog fights but I was hunting with Ben Williams who has spent some time as a professional dog trainer and we walked in with confidence. I still have a scar on my leg to prove I tried. Ben got it through the hand and the whole thing turned into a bloody mess. We finally broke it up but neither dog was satisfied and to the day Kelly died we had to watch them closely.

As we patched up our wounds, Ben remarked that there had been times when Kelly was winning. Then he repeated the old saying:

"It's not the size of the dog in the fight. It's the size of the fight in the dog!"

A little mutt with fire can go awfully good for a while. Somebody let a yellow Lab get too close to Kelly's dish one time and Kelly had him pretty badly chewed up before we stopped it. Of course once the Lab got started Kelly would have been only a tidbit. I'm really not bragging about having a fighting dog but it was hard not to admire the little rascal.

"He'd have made a hell of a football player," a coach once told me.

But like other dogs who live with people and without other dogs around constantly, Kelly turned into something of a prima donna. He didn't eat very much and during hunting season we worried a little about it. Give him a doggie bone and he'd trot around and show it to everybody, then put it away somewhere.

Ben Williams, the aforementioned expert, visited our house one time when Kelly was ignoring his heaped dish.

"Trouble is," Ben said, "he has no competition for food and he enjoys being coddled and coaxed. Makes him feel important. Watch this."

So Ben got down on hands and knees and approached Kelly's dish. Kelly suddenly became attentive. His eyes popped. His tail stiffened.

Ben stopped at the dish and stuck his head down toward it.

"Slurp, glub, glub," said Ben.

Kelly looked at me in amazement and back at Ben. Ben got up and walked away. Kelly hurried to the dish and ate the whole thing rapidly with his eyes rolling apprehensively. This was a gratifying experience for me: it proved conclusively that we were just as smart as Kelly, maybe smarter.

Now if you are going to haul a dog all over the country to hunt all of those birds you need a good traveler. When Kelly was quite young we got him a Miami Beach towel. It had palm trees and "Miami Beach" in big letters and Kelly soon learned he was supposed to stay on that towel when living in motels. As time went on he learned that as long as he could touch the towel everything was all right. He would take a pretty long lead like a guy edging off first base but when anyone looked at him he'd tag up again.

As the years went by Kelly learned that he could leave his towel with impunity when he was alone. Oh, he'd never get on a bed or anything that would leave any incriminating evidence but when you came back you'd hear him scramble to tag up again. The towel was getting pretty well worn when Kelly left us just before he was eight years old, but he never nibbled it or scratched it. That towel was important, even when he was a pup and a little hard on other softies he found lying around.

There are pointing specialists who learn only one or two birds. Kelly would point to anything after he learned we wanted it, but he always felt big birds were better. The toughest time I had keeping him in line was when I'd hunt valley quail (California quail) in chukar country.

The chukar is a cackling rascal who lives in the high, dry mountain country, sometimes adjacent to the bottoms and draws where quail stay. If Kelly was tending to business with the quail and happened to hear a chukar call he'd slip off, going faster and faster, and head for the high places. Chukar were bigger and hence more important. After a little I'd see him parading around on a hillside trying to get me to follow him and the chukars.

And old Kelly would point woodcock. It took him only an hour or so to learn that business despite what folks say about the timberdoodle smelling different and having no attraction for dogs that haven't been trained for them.

The man I first went woodcock hunting with was a loyal pointer man and a good one, who asked if that little fuzzy dog would point birds. I didn't impress him with my answer and he figured my dog was going to be a nuisance. The pointers tended to put him down, too.

Well, Kelly found a woodcock and a big handsome pointer backed him momentarily and then hunkered down and sneaked past Kelly like a Walt Disney animated snake. When the big pointer had passed Kelly, he stood up and stole the point. The pointer's owner walked in, kicked up the bird and downed it, called "Fetch!" and complimented me on my dog.

"That little fuzzy dog sure backs good," he said.

Thanks a lot.

A while later my new friend's big pointers failed to find a woodcock that was evidently trundling around in a grassy patch. After considerable careful shuffling they went off. Along came Kelly, operating on his own, checked the grass patch and nailed the woodcock. My friend kicked it up and shot it.

"That little fuzzy dog's tired," he said. "I'm going to put him back in the car."

He did and Kelly spent the rest of the afternoon trying to dismantle the dog box and yelling bloody murder. Being banished was the final insult of a day of injustices.

It took me several years to shoot all of the upland birds of North America over Kelly. It started out by accident, and then I suddenly realized I had most of them and began to plan special trips.

Long ago Kelly went to where I like to think all of the bones are juicy and the birds never flush wild. They say a man is entitled to one good hunting dog in a lifetime. I guess I've had mine.

When I was a kid the dogs were supposed to look like arrows with head and tail making one straight line. Although I realize that an upright tail is more likely to show above the brush, the old-fashioned way always seemed more exciting.

Chapter Six

It's Tradition

Even *The American Field* does it. *The American Field* is the recognized authority on pointing field trials and just below the masthead on its front are two dogs pointing together. One is an English pointer and the other an English setter. The setter is backing the pointer.

As I studied it the other day it occurred to me that I cannot recall much art work in which the setter is not backing the pointer. Traditionally, I guess, an artist is supposed to do it that way. Now in *The American Field* there may be a reason. Pointers win more field trials than setters do and it is natural, I guess, for the pointer to make the find and for the setter to show respect. But the same pecking order is carried out in a few thousand sporting prints and all sorts of bird dog book illustrations. It goes way back. I have a little porcelain of a pointer and a setter pointing and I am sure you can guess which one is ahead. No telling how old that porcelain is.

Anyway, the hunting dog business is traditional, even though the traditions change from time to time. For example, the modern setter or pointer, whether winning a field trial or locating a woodcock in some woodlot, is supposed to carry his tail high. He is also supposed to keep his head high.

When I was a kid the dogs were supposed to look like arrows with head and tail making one straight line. Although I realize that an upright tail is more likely to show above the brush, the old-fashioned way always seemed more exciting.

Now I never have been sold on the high head for all situations since I know that the scent may be pretty close to the ground. I always figured that it tended to move quite a bit like smoke and if there's a high wind a dog might smell a chokecherry bush instead of a grouse sitting under it as long as he didn't get his head down to the bird's level.

High-headed dogs are supposed to be seeking body scent instead of the odds and ends that might be snuffled off the bushes. The ground trailer becomes a pariah of the bird dog business although I submit humbly that there are some species of birds likely to travel great distances on the ground and body scent might be a bit scarce if the subject is something like 300 yards away. About all the dog has to work with is what the bird left. But then, most of those who set the traditional behavior patterns usually hunt where there are enough birds that trailing one over the ridge is a waste of time. Anyway, I think that's how it is.

So I look at somebody's old grouse dog "puttering" as the field trial people say. And then I look at a wild animal, a pronghorn or a coyote, lowering and lifting his head when he sights something strange—feeling for the proper level to get the best scent—and I figure he just isn't with it. The complimentary description of a top pointer is "high at both ends!"

Jack and I got one of the collars. For crude, old-fashioned dog owners who have never seen an electric collar, I shall explain. There is a collar you put on the dog and it has a couple of contact points that push against his neck. You carry a little gadget with a collapsible aerial in a holster on your belt. When you push the red button it stings a dog out to almost half a mile. Since Danny did half a mile rather quickly, I practiced a fast draw.

Chapter Seven

In Pursuit of a Good Bird Dog

They ran Danny with a 20-foot checkcord streaming behind him, which should have been an omen. He was a six-month-old setter, almost entirely white, and let's face it: Danny was a field-trial castoff, his parents being seasoned campaigners of impeccable credentials.

Now I know about field-trial dogs and would never expect to follow one on my ancient legs when they are bred to be handled by people on good horses, but Danny was the age of pup I wanted and the breeder figured he wouldn't be a big goer. He also didn't hold his tail quite high enough for the field-trial business. I found later that Danny held his tail low for more effective streamlining, using it as a sort of spoiler.

Danny is not the first speedster I have owned. For a couple of years I tried to keep track of a lantern-jawed pointer named Murphy. You may have seen him passing your place at one time or another, for I have no idea where he hunted when I couldn't see him.

Murphy was very tiring. He had a propensity for becoming lost, only to stand around and yap for me—not that I could catch him when I found him—he just wanted to keep things organized and would, upon seeing me, take off again. He was a picturesque pointer occasionally, but I was seldom able to reach him before the birds went off to feed, and generally I could not even determine what species Murphy had found. I gave Murphy away, after which he won a national prairie-chicken championship in Alberta—where most of the birds are sharptail grouse.

Since I once watched Murphy run up 320 acres of sage grouse without stopping, I read with interest the account of his championship in the *American Field*. It seems the judges had been a little puzzled since on one occasion Murphy disappeared over a distant ridge, whereupon quite a number of birds took off from somewhere way out there. The *American*

Field reporter said there was no way of proving that Murphy had flushed the birds, so only Murphy and I know what really happened and at this late date I see no reason for being a snitch. Back to Danny.

As soon as I got Danny home and took him out of the crate I threw a dummy for him and he retrieved it with the solemnity of a real pro, thus cementing our friendship. It was a nice gesture on his part, although he hasn't done it since.

My wife and I took Danny out to run on a broad field, and remembering the procedure at his home kennel, I left a 20-foot checkcord attached to his collar. When I turned him loose, he left.

I was not with Debie when she caught him, as she beat me to the car. She didn't have much trouble, she said, and collared him on the highway between DeLand, Florida and New Smyrna Beach, with the aid of some truck drivers who helped to corner him against a fence. She said the station wagon would run faster than Danny but he could turn quicker.

Things worked fine the second workout because Danny accidentally ran through some rodeo grounds and got confused among the chutes. All I did was vault scratchily over a board fence topped with barbed wire and I had him cornered. Each time I'd catch him he would greet me with enthusiasm and try to sit on my lap on the way home.

Then I found a beautiful place for him to run—a weedy strip bounded by a fence on one side and a deep canal on the other. As a steadying influence I put him down with Tex, my conventionally paced and controllable old Brittany. That was at five P.M. on a cooling Florida evening in spring. At three A.M. the next morning I was awakened by Danny's bell. I had been sleeping in the station wagon and he was coming down a moonlit sand trail, accompanied by Tex. Tex eyed me with apprehension, but Danny treated the event as a routine workout.

That ended Danny's Florida exercise, as we were heading out West soon and I figured a few thousand acres of sagebrush would fit Danny's lifestyle because he'd soon have to realize we were all in this bird-hunting business together. When I first turned him loose in the sage I observed with pride how he quartered ahead of me, and I was not really apprehensive until I saw him through my binoculars, topping out a mile away on a grassy ridge.

Half an hour later he was coming straight back toward me and I was sure he'd had his little wind sprint and was ready to settle down; but while I blasted on the whistle and screamed promises of raw steak and a new doghouse he passed me full bore at a distance of 20 yards without turning his head and did a couple of miles in the opposite direction. This recurred on several occasions and at the end of approximately three hours he would come to the truck—not to me, the truck. I couldn't catch him 20 feet from it, but when we both got in we were buddies again. The rendezvous had to be in the truck.

It was the second time out that we got into the coyote bit. As Danny dipped over the third ridge I heard the yaps of a coyote, and then another, and I wondered what was going on.

"Watch it!" a local rancher said. "Coyotes sometimes kill our young stock dogs."

The next time out I had an athletic young friend with me and when the coyote chorus started he ran off in that direction. Not to worry, he reported. The coyotes chased Danny but Danny paid no attention to them and after a quarter mile the tired wolves just sat down and barked at him.

I tried a change of territory and released Danny in the foothills, headed uphill, figuring gravity might bring him back. An hour later I climbed a knob and with binoculars sighted him in a canyon. He was playing tag with a black bear, but he came in shortly after that.

It was about that time we began to discuss the electric collar. Bird season was coming and Danny and I had no agreement yet. I'd heard about electric collars for a long time and the last word was that Murphy's attention had finally been gained with one. I understand that part of our energy shortage is due to the juice needed to light him up.

Some of my information on electric collars was pretty old, and I knew they had been improved. Trainers called them everything from the hand of God to instruments of torture. But very brief shocks might be the answer for Danny. Or would Danny just speed up?

One of my informants told me he had used an electric collar to break his pointer of chasing rabbits. When the pointer would refuse to stop a chase he would get a little jolt of electricity.

"I broke him of chasing rabbits," the man said, "but it is kind of embarrassing. Now whenever my dog sees a rabbit he rolls over on his back and howls."

It was along here that Charley came into the picture. Charley is a pint-sized Brittany owned by Jack Ward and we may as well face it—Charley is a cow chaser. Charley was named after me and at first I was flattered.

Jack and I wondered how an electric collar would affect Charley's impromptu herding instincts. One collar could be used with both Danny and Charley, we reasoned. The real decision came when Charley added a new wrinkle to his cow chasing. On that day he would chase a cow for a few yards and then run back to us at top speed and tear around and around us just out of reach, barking loudly, while we said things like, "You shouldn't do that, Charley!"

Jack and I got one of the collars. For crude, old-fashioned dog owners who have never seen an electric collar, I shall explain. There is a collar you put on the dog and it has a couple of contact points that push against his neck. You carry a little gadget with a collapsible aerial in a holster on your belt. When you push the red button it stings a dog out to almost half a mile. Since Danny did half a mile rather quickly, I practiced a fast draw.

"I am not going to bust my dog with this thing until I know how strong it is," Jack announced firmly. "We've gotta test it."

I asked him how and he thought a minute, then said to leave that to him. The next day he told me that he had made the test and the collar was fine. It had considerable shock, he said, but was not going to knock Charley into a coma. In the interest of science I inquired.

"I had George over last night to show him the collar," Jack said, "and when he had hold of it just right, I hit the button. Well, George jumped out of his chair and I think his hair sort of stood up. You know, perhaps we shouldn't mention to him that it was not an accident."

Anyhow, after a couple of jolts Charley pretended not to notice cattle, although you could see him watching them out of the corner of his eye, obviously looking for their concealed weapons.

We took Danny to a freshly disked field that seemed to extend clear off the earth's surface. This was in Montana where the ranchers don't like to turn their tractors too much. I tested the collar with the little light-up gadget before I put it on and while it was being installed Danny maintained his usual appearance of friendly nonchalance.

I turned him loose and he started across the field, little spurts of dust behind him and a long way apart. I yelled "Whoa!" twice. Although this would stop Danny in his tracks in the back yard, it was only a formality in the field. I also blew the whistle.

Then I pushed the button and there was a cloud of dust where Danny had been. The dust exuded a couple of yips and Danny came out of it headed for protection. Since I was standing up he could not jump on my lap, but he gave evidence of wishing to communicate.

The truck was only a few yards away and just as I told him to load up, Danny decided he must have been mistaken the first time so he smoked off in another direction. I yelled and blew the whistle and then touched the button and Danny homed in on me, then looked back toward where he'd come from. There was, he seemed to feel, something out there.

Not wanting to keep Danny wired for the rest of his life, I put a bell on his electric collar so he would associate that with the unpleasantness that happened when he went too far. Then, with a little use of a dummy electric collar, also carrying a bell, I figured I'd have it made. There was one complication.

When Danny was out of sight I didn't dare touch the button for fear he might be on point or even heading in, and after bird season opened I did considerable sprinting for high vantage points. Most of our hunting was for Hungarian partridge in a single area, as I thought familiarity with the terrain might help me find him in an emergency. The emergencies occurred regularly.

The country is a series of ravines leading up to Sheep Mountain which bulges out of the high grass country. The coulees are grassy, with clumps of cottonwood and occasional aspens, and the Huns have been there every year.

Resting Huns are generally along the edges of the draws where the cover is not too thick, sometime in their standard coveys of a dozen or so birds, sometimes scattered in two's and three's, and occasionally bunched up in larger groups. When a dog points one of the big bunches and I walk them up, they're likely to divide up with each of the original coveys heading toward its home territory. About half the time the Huns get up wild anyway—the adult Hun not being noted as a good dog-training subject, generally standing in grass thin enough that he can observe a dog's progress, his apprehension building while he discusses the situation with his buddies.

Coveys are apt to be a considerable distance apart and I would not say such hunting is conducive to reducing Danny's range, but since I didn't have any pen-raised quail I had to go with the Huns, or rather somewhat behind them.

On the muzzleloader day I had started out fairly early, in the futile hope of tiring Danny a little. He was wearing his electric collar and his bell jangled busily through the little brush patches but we didn't find any birds for a while and that was my undoing.

I'd heard some thumping noises a long way off toward the mountain and when I found a pair of specks and put my binoculars on them it developed there were a couple of muzzleloader Hun hunters over there, doing considerable shooting, each shot marked by a white bloom of smoke. It was a little later that Danny and his tinkle disappeared. The whistle did no good, so after a couple of hours I headed to where I thought I might intercept the lads with the charcoal burners.

They hadn't seen any dog, they said, but they looked at each other, appearing a little relieved. Did my dog have a bell, they wanted to know. It seems they had been hearing a mysterious tinkling in the draws all around them but had never sighted anything. I assured them that the muzzleloaders hadn't started their heads ringing. By that time, however, the tinkling had ceased and at dark I went back to town to get the camping equipment I use when Danny makes one of his wider casts. My wife wasn't home and as I went into the darkened house I decided my six months of Danny had been enough. I was tired, and through the back of my groggy brain ran the faint tinkle of Danny's bell. I shook my head violently and it stopped.

I got the sleeping bag, wrote a note and grabbed a couple of cans of Vienna sausage and a box of crackers and headed for the door, disturbed when I seemed again to hear a shred of ghostly tinkle. I shook my head and it did not stop. This I considered a bad sign.

The phone rang and I dropped the box of crackers in reaching for it.

"Did you find your dog?" came a solicitous voice. "This is one of the guys with the muzzleloaders."

"Nope," I said. "I'm going out there again now."

"Try your kennel," the man said. "We put him in there."

Danny was there, all right, his bell notes carrying faintly to the house. He'd finally checked in with the strangers, evidently assuming that anyone he chose would bring him home. The next time he got lost I sat down on a hill at dusk and fired three dollars worth of shotgun shells into the air. Danny's spirit-like white form finally materialized from a deep arroyo.

"If I ever kill a bird over that clown, I'll buy him a steak!" I promised Debie, mentally adding up the initial cost, the dog food, vet bills, some kennel fees and the 300-dollar electric collar.

I took Danny out to the wheatfields when the mountain shadows were stretching and the winding wet-weather creeks that cut through the big fields looked like jagged black slashes in the yellow stubble. At evening the Huns drift out into the fields to feed, and in a field I can see Danny.

Danny sprinted along one of the draws, showing mild interest in a jackrabbit while I fingered the button but never pushed it. He checked the other side of the ditch and then seemed magnetized toward the open field. He went with his head high and his tail went up, too. Then he stopped suddenly, cat-walked 15 feet and did the whole number, head high, white tail like a plume and the intent look in his eye that would have pleased his folks.

I stumbled up a little to one side so he could see me and was even with his nose when the Huns twittered up, a little far out but within range, and they swung hard right, followed by the gun muzzle, which it seemed would never catch up. One bird and let the others go, I told myself, just as if I habitually make doubles. Bang!

The bird came down hard, a pair of feathers hanging in the air, and Danny ran a little way and watched the others out of sight. Then he found the dead one and ran around aimlessly with it. That, of course, I told myself, was a retrieve.

I was a little surprised somehow to find it was just like any other Hun. I would not have been surprised if it had carried a silver plate with Danny's registration number on it. It had been a long, hard way and I suppose I should have announced to the world that I had a setter that would do it all.

But I have viewed these miraculous things before. That was last year. This season he may have retired from bird hunting entirely.

"They just keep flying into this field every afternoon,"
Harry said. "Do you just shoot them going or coming
or do you scare them before you shoot? This doesn't
look very sporting."

I told Harry to hide near the field and shoot them
both going and coming.

Chapter Eight

How to Shoot Doves

Harry was raised in a state where doves are songbirds and he is a waterfowl hunter. He is a Labrador-retriever-using, sneakboat-sneaking, camouflage-wearing, 300-decoy water-fowler. He shoots a hand-made duck gun that cost twice as much as my car, and he shoots it pretty good.

I went duck hunting with Harry and learned that he doesn't take easy shots. Harry said it was unsportsmanlike to shoot a decoying pintail with its feet reaching for the water. I'd always figured it was fair as long as their toes weren't wet. Harry said you shoot at ducks only between 30 and 55 yards. Other ranges are unsportsmanlike, he said. He said never to shoot a hen. I was so busy trying to discern distances and sex that I didn't do very well. Harry shot his limit but felt very bad because he had to fire twice at a blue-winged teal that towered directly into the sun.

Harry made a great deal of money in a state where they don't shoot doves, and when he got down into dove country he was disappointed that duck hunters down here don't use jet boats like the one he had up north. He thought an airboat was less fun. He said that, frankly, there seemed to be fewer ducks down here than there were up where he came from.

I hunted doves with Harry by telephone. He asked me about dove shooting and wanted to know if the doves we shoot are the same ones that walk around his bird feeder and make friendly noises. He wanted to know if adults hunt them or if they are only a training bird for youngsters. I told him that many dove shooters are adults, although they often act a little childish, and the next time he called he said he had the doves located—in fact, he had bought the land they were feeding on.

"They just keep flying into this field every afternoon," Harry said. "Do you just shoot them going or coming or do you scare them before you shoot? This doesn't look very sporting."

I told Harry to hide near the field and shoot them both going and coming. I said that he should build a blind if he wanted to do it right and that he should invite some of his friends to keep the birds moving. He asked if doves were really good to eat and said he was sorry I couldn't be there to explain the finer points. I told him to rest the field for several days after shooting it or the doves would leave. I don't think he was listening very well, but he asked me what gun to use. I said it depended on how the birds were flying and that improved cylinder and modified would be good for the double guns he used. He said he would take a matched pair of Perazzis with interchangeable choke tubes.

I didn't hear any more from Harry until four days after the season opened, and when he called I asked him how the dove hunt had gone.

"I killed my limit," Harry said. Then there was a rather long pause and Harry said "I used 108 shells. Bird of peace, hell!"

Doves are different and kind of hard to hit. The first time I went dove shooting they put me facing some high trees, and the birds came over so fast I didn't know what I was doing, but I shot pretty well. The second time I figured it out, got in a better place and would have starved if we hadn't had some lasagna at home. The hardest dove to hit is one that you watch for a long time and swing on very carefully, picking him up and following him in (and out).

I think good dove shooters are the best game shots in the world and that they're better than the old market shooters ever were, even though I couldn't prove it. Some of the old-timers of the golden age of shotgunning really stacked up the feathered folk, but there are American dove bangers who go down into Latin America and shoot as long as they can see over their heaps of game. No complaint on that because doves are farm pests in those areas.

The best average on doves that I ever watched was made by a hotshot tennis player who evidently had "sharply honed reflexes," as the sportswriters say. This deadeye showed up at a dove shoot and was stationed with his autoloader at the edge of the field beside a tall, dead tree. Dove veterans, of course, know that a single dead tree at the edge of a dove field is likely to be the objective of all manner of suspicious doves that home in on it with the idea of alighting to inspect the facilities. As far as I could tell, the well-hidden marksman with the autoloader missed only one dove all afternoon. It was flying past at about 30 yards. All of the others he shot had sat down in the tree.

In my observation, and second only to the tennis expert by the dead tree, the most doves per box of shells were collected by a fellow who used a very large Labrador retriever, an accommodating fellow who retrieved all birds dropped by everybody in the area to his owner. The Lab's policy was that all birds should be gathered into one pile and be divided after the shoot was over. Although this system was not approved by all shooters, the Lab would growl loudly in friendly fashion when a stranger asked him for a bird. His master not only got his limit with expenditure of few shells but never had any badly shotup birds. My only explanation is that he chose his range with great care. Or possibly he was so good he took close-in shots only with the edge of his pattern.

The matter of shooting distance is pretty important and most of the good shooters will have some sort of range marker out there to indicate whether the birds are close enough or not. Good shots generally put it at 40 yards and others mark it at 30 yards. I set it at 12 yards and would bait it if that weren't illegal. I left one shoot early when I realized I was the range marker for the fellow 30 yards to my left.

Location on a dove field is pretty important, of course. Not many dove shooters really build blinds; most of them just wear camouflange clothing. Most of the shooters stand around the edges although some of the best shooting can be in the center of the field where birds are really trying to put down to feed if they have survived the border patrol.

There are plenty of reasons given for doves being hard to hit, including speed, variable winds and careless flying, but there are some other things. For example, most flying doves are not very close to stationary objects on the ground and we have no point of reference. Thus, we squint up into the sky at a bird that has a great many forward gears (the rumor that a dove can go into reverse in calm air is unfounded) and have nothing but a wavering shotgun barrel with which to judge its momentum and course.

Not only have we no sure way of gauging the bird's speed and direction but its course can change subtly as it stares down into a dark hole with a charge of No. 7½ chilled shot at the bottom. A large share of the angles have changed while we mount a gun and swing it—and we don't always notice that. Ducks are different. I doubt if a dove can match the speed of a ringbill diving power-on, and it probably can't change direction as fast as a green-winged teal, but doves are mentally unstable and alter objective repeatedly while I punch a safety, stab a barrel and yank a trigger.

Speed? Well, in calm air and going somewhere but with no gunfire astern, a dove is likely to fly at about 37 to 40 miles an hour, according to various speedometers I have used on country roads. If you add that to a 50-mile-an-hour tail-wind, it is better not to dwell on the total—and if you add another 10 or 15 miles an hour for haste during shooting, the thing gets a little out of hand. My friend Joe is a pretty fair shotgun shover and tells of the time he shot doves beside a sheltering row of trees and lacked only three for his limit, having missed hardly any and feeling pretty sportsmanlike. It was a high-wind day and he decided to go out into an unprotected area to finish up. Out there the birds were riding a 40-mile whistler. Joe went back to the trees while he still had enough shells left to complete his limit.

I relate that epic to show that one day's score on doves should not be carved in stone. Most dove shooting is a series of good runs and some bad days when there is question about the ammunition. Much of the worst missing results from misjudgment, tricky wind, especially spooky doves or all three. Hitting a dove is very simple. So is walking a tight wire or lifting a refrigerator. It's the execution that gets you.

Most good shots use the swing-through method of coming up behind the bird and pulling the trigger as the muzzle goes past, the extra speed of swing taking care of most of the lead. Most coaches recommend this to all game shooters, whatever they say about trap or skeet. However, some of the best dove shots change procedures with the range. One of the finest I know uses a sustained lead (measuring the forward allowance and holding it at the bird's flight speed as he pulls the trigger) at long range, although he uses the swing-through at short range. He also uses two guns—a fast little 20 gauge double when the ranges are to be short and a 12-gauge trapgun for long-haul shooting. He kills some 50-yard doves, but most of us should find something else to do while they are passing that far away. I generally count my shells or look for my sandwich.

Telling people how to hit doves makes me uncomfortable and I hasten to mention that all instruction is borrowed from good shots and none of it is my idea. The really good shooters generally haven't the slightest idea of how the hell they do it and getting them to think about it will ruin their whole season. They agree on one thing: when you see a dove coming at a distance, don't start swinging on him until you're ready to shoot. Being too careful is a sure miss. Let your instincts take over. My instincts tell me to stay away from dove fields.

Nobody knows whether it's a good dove year or a bad year—except in the areas where he hunts. Biological surveys tend to come up with one firm summary: there are a heck of a lot of doves.

We have resident doves that spend their lives in one area. We also have migratory doves that are heading south because it was too cold where they came from. And we also have migratory doves that are heading north because it was warmer than they expected where they've been. We have southbound doves that stop for the winter and northbound doves that stop off because it is better than where they went when they went south earlier. We have doves that are fed up with the setup and just leave. This means that dove shooting can be anything from terrific to lousy, but no one will know why for a season, and by that time everything will have changed anyway. The game managers do say that although we shoot millions of doves, we don't seem to affect the overall populaton, and states with no open seasons don't seem to gain numbers.

Any time a couple of doves have time on their hands they build a nest and produce more doves. It is said that this may happen as many as six times during a year, the whole procedure taking a little more than a month. Unless we become better shots or work harder at it, three or four million dove shooters can't make much impression.

Doves generally feed twice a day, once early in the morning after getting off the roost and then around mid-afternoon to evening. In between, if they aren't nesting, they sit around in trees or on telephone wires and watch what happens, generally looking surprised. Flocking is generally pretty loose and a dove formation is short on discipline, only the Wilson's snipe seeming less organized. In the case of the snipe I feel it is a matter of stubborn individuality. In the case of the dove I believe it's a matter of just not paying attention.

Waterhole gunning is quite different from operations at most Florida dove fields. Doves go to water after eating and I've seen some pretty easy marks when they dropped in near well-concealed shooters—but sometimes they dive in mighty fast with their wings folded. Except for isolated incidents already mentioned, the best scores I have seen were made when doves were fluttering down for a drink and thought they were alone.

Waterhole shooting is most popular in some of the arid Western states. Stock "tanks" (out there a stock *pond* is a "tank," which makes it a little confusing when you're thinking of one made out of sheet metal) may be located so far from other standing water that they attract birds from a wide area.

It is south of here where individuals make the biggest bags, the mourning doves concentrating through funnel-shaped Central America and carrying leg bands from many of our states. Down there, shooters (mostly from the South) can burn about as many shells as they like and you'll meet some of the world's best. That's where you can find out just how good the top shooters are.

Political problems have made Central and South American dove shooting a stop-and-go proposition recently, but there's always Mexican shooting.

Since dove hunters do a lot of shooting, guns and shells are important subjects. For years I read that a dainty 20- or 28-gauge was just nifty for doves. Since doves aren't particularly hard to kill, light guns are routine recommendations, but they have their disadvantages if you're going to shoot 50 shells in Florida or 250 in Honduras. The recoil you didn't notice at all on quail or ducks suddenly builds up as the day goes along.

Dove shooters often choose gas-operated autoloaders for the reduced kick—and since there's seldom much walking involved there's no particular need for lightweight guns. Even a 7½-pound autoloader can become a bit wearing after a hundred heavy loads are fired—part of them when the gun is hurriedly and incorrectly mounted. This isn't skeet shooting.

I found myself in Honduras when someone (the ammunition for those shoots is brought through the armed forces) had decided that 1¼-ounce loads would be better than the one-ouncers usually used there in 12-gauge. After the second day there were quite a few walking wounded, and even the auto shooters were padding their shoulders with everything from hotel towels to foam rubber.

For long-experienced shooters I'd say a modified barrel throwing at least an ounce of shot is about perfect for most doves. That could be 12, 16 or 20 gauge. The 28-gauge, which somehow patterns beyond its apparent capabilities, is used by good shots at close-in birds. For wild and experienced birds at long range, some will go to full-choked guns and 1¼ ounces of 7½ shot.

Generally, nothing but a pattern sheet will show what these guns are really doing. I have checked modified barrels that threw cylinder patterns and have always felt the fellow who engraves the choke designation on the barrels should get acquainted with whoever bores them. Believe me, patterns are important on doves. Except for a bundle of gray feathers there isn't much there.

I had a friend with a remarkable record on distant doves. He shot a Model 12 Winchester pump that everyone figured was about as near a rifle as you could get with a wad of shot. I borrowed it and checked it out. It threw 67 per cent patterns, which is barely full choke by most definitions. Maybe that's about as tight as even a good shot can handle consistently on doves.

Beginning shooters should forego tight bores and long shots. Improved cylinder choke is about right. They'd be better off with No. 8 shot, 7½'s when using tighter barrels. Some dove shooters use skeet borings and small shot—but they wait for the close ones. Don't use big shot with skeet choke or improved cylinder choke.

I questioned a good dove shooter who was getting on in years and aware of it. He adjusted his guns and shooting accordingly. He said that as a youth he had used nothing but full-choked guns and simply "waited them out" if the birds got too close. Then as he got older, with poorer eyesight and reflexes, he had gradually used more open guns until he settled on improved cylinder. He doesn't take long shots anymore.

Note that this is the exact opposite of the quail shooters who go to tighter borings as they get slower. Quail are generally going away instead of—well, whatever doves do.

I have bought guns, handloaded special ammunition, read books on dove biology and traveled considerable distances to catch them unprepared. As nearly as I can tell from the census estimates I have not changed the dove totals much.

*My old Brittany Tex (guess where he was raised)
turned into a pretty good bird dog, but he wouldn't
retrieve. He'd hunt long and hard if necessary for a
dead bird, but when he found it, he'd carry it off and
drop it—maybe 40 or 50 feet away. He would never
find it again for me, no matter how hard I pleaded or
threatened. I had to do that myself while he looked on
encouragingly as if he were proud of my progress.*

Chapter Nine

Fetch

Dogs are supposed to bring things. They bring ducks, quail, frisbees and house slippers to other people. They don't bring much to me. This retrieving business, however, can be profitable. My friend Carl got into retrieving a couple of years ago and borrowed my electric collar to train his Labrador. I figured Carl didn't know too much about dogs and so I gave him considerable instruction in use of the collar. The way he goes into things I figured his dog would look like a neon sign after a couple of days.

He paid $250 for the pup, which he told me didn't work out. So Carl sold it for $1,500 and bought his own electric collar. Then he got two more Labs, a golden retriever and a springer spaniel. He said the golden and the springer weren't making it so he sold them. I figured Carl just didn't have the touch for dog training, even though he was showing a profit.

Then I got a call from Carl in which, among other things, he mentioned that he had sold his Lab and gotten another one. I wasn't paying much attention, figuring here was a guy who never would be satisfied with any dog.

"A field trial man made me an offer I couldn't refuse," Carl said. "He gave me $49,000."

I asked Carl to repeat what he had just said because there have been some telephone problems since the system breakup. He'd said $49,000 all right. Now, Carl and his dogs are real and so is the $49,000. Carl is not his real name though. He bought his wife a Porsche.

Back in caveman days I suppose there were retrievers same as now, and although dinosaurs are too heavy, I am sure there were all sorts of birds and beasties for the dogs to fetch. The retrieving instinct, if it is an instinct, has been developed since then but it does not always work out. Regarding retrieving, dogs have individual ideas, few of them involving bringing birds to me.

Some dogs are selfish about birds in the hand—or rather in the mouth. My friend George bought a mail-order pointer of impeccable breeding and invited me to watch him try it out. It pointed beautifully, and when the birds flew George spilled one in a patch of brush and marked the others down off to the left.

Sultan, the dog, dashed into the brush after the dead bird while George moved toward the others, and after Sultan stayed gone for a while, George suggested I go in and see if he was having trouble finding the bird. Sultan was just sitting in there when I found him, but I saw no bird, and George followed me in and said he guessed that one was lost. Sultan burped politely.

Then Sultan pointed once more like a field trial champion, and George scored again. This time, when we went into the brush after Sultan, it was quite noticeable that he had quail feathers sticking to his mouth. When George shot a third quail, I was amazed at the speed with which he beat Sultan to it.

Before he went home, George said he had gotten his feet wet and that he was going to change shoes and socks at the truck. Sultan watched him take off a boot and drop his damp sock on the grass. Sultan swallowed the sock and looked hopefully at the other boot.

"You know," George said, "I doubt if I ever do break that dog of eating birds!"

The sock and Sultan were real. That is not George's real name.

I had two friends named Jack and Jerry (real names) who got a highly-touted and expensive German Shorthair by mail-order from a southern kennel. They had him on two weeks' trial, and they lived way up north where seasons open early. After the dog ate all of Jack's and Jerry's birds, the seller had to take it back. Jack commented, however, that such a dog was a very easy keeper, requiring hardly any dog food.

Joe's pointer, Lady, was one of those reliable, conscientious dogs who takes her work seriously. She was retrieving a quail for Joe when he hauled off with his old Fox and shot another one, which she encountered on the way back in. Now there are stories of dogs pointing birds with others in their mouths and there are stories of dogs bringing in two at once, but Lady had never studied those programs and she was confronted with what the military experts might term a problem in logistics. Here she was with one bird in her mouth and another bird that she wanted to take to Joe too.

After a brief survey of the situation with several changes of expression, Lady gulped hard, swallowing bird number one, and triumphantly turned toward Joe with bird number two in her mouth. But halfway in, while mentally reviewing the situation, Lady concluded she had done wrong. A look of canine consternation came to her face and she apologetically crawled the last 20 feet on her stomach.

Really fine retrievers are pretty good thinkers. McGillicuddy was a small Brittany who felt game should be divided equally. When his owner Ben and I were jumpshooting ducks along a narrow creek, Ben spilled two mallards on the other side, while I didn't get a shot because of intervening brush. McGillicuddy, who had crouched in the background while we stalked the spot, crossed the creek and sloshed far out into the boggy area to get them. Ben waded across after him.

McGillicuddy brought one duck to Ben and returned to look for the second, which he finally found and started back with, barely able to travel in deep mud and water while trying to hold up the big bird. He could not see where he was going very well.

"Good dog!" said Ben, and reached for the bird. McGillicuddy skipped splashily to one side and avoided him, whereupon Ben made some rather frank statements about retrieving in general and McGillicuddy in particular. But old Mac turned back toward the creek, swam across it with the duck and looked for me on the other side. I hadn't crossed, and when he found me (he was staring over and around one of the bird's wings), he brought me the duck. That made everything even, and as the bedraggled Mac shook himself, I could have sworn he said, "Whew!"

Determination is important in retrievers. I went to a field trial where a big Lab was sent to get a trussed-up duck. Some fellows way out there in a boat would fire in the air and toss a bird into the water. The dog, waiting on shore some distance away, was to go get the bird and bring it in, but the duck somehow swam under a part of the boat and the dog couldn't find it. Not being easily discouraged, the pooch then climbed into the boat despite remonstrations from its occupants, and grabbed the crate of ducks. But even a big Lab in a bad humor has trouble with a whole crate of mallards, so he stopped and ripped one of the boards loose to get at the ducks inside. His owner finally got him stopped. The dog looked disgusted and glared at the gallery.

I got an early impression of retrievers when a friend would mark an orange with his fingernail and then throw it on top of a truck full of oranges. Then he'd call his Labrador, who would climb onto the truck, pick up the marked orange and bring it back. Good demonstration, although I have since learned that the strong human scent makes this easy for a dog with a good nose.

You will note that such instances of brilliant retrieving in-volve other people's dogs. When I buy a dog it immediately resigns from retrieving. The last one I got was a Brittany that was the showoff specialist for a well-known kennel. He'd retrieve anything he was asked to, and his owner was in the process of teaching him to put dead birds in his coat. His name is Spike and he does not bring birds to me, although he frequently presents me with his squeaky toy.

So I set up what they call a retrieving table—a long one, waist-high with a trolley wire you attach the dog to. Then you fasten a string to the dog's toe, and when you twitch it a little it is uncomfortable and the dog opens his mouth, whereupon you stick a retrieving dummy into it and say, "Fetch!" With more practice the dog will pick up the dummy from the table at increasing distances, and bring it to you along the trolley. Spike took to this process with enthusiasm, and the next step was to have him bring the dummy from the ground. He didn't care much for that. He wants to do it on the table, and when he gets near it, he yelps and tries to climb onto it. He never learned that the table is supposed to be the unpleasant part. He won't bring me birds.

My old Brittany Tex (guess where he was raised) turned into a pretty good bird dog, but he wouldn't retrieve. He'd hunt long and hard if necessary for a dead bird, but when he found it, he'd carry it off and drop it—maybe 40 or 50 feet away. He would never find it again for me, no matter how hard I pleaded or threatened. I had to do that myself while he looked on encouragingly as if he were proud of my progress.

Kelly, another Brittany, wouldn't retrieve anything he thought I could find. On a venture into the North, I shot a big cock pheasant that landed on short grass, looking something like a crashed bomber. Kelly hadn't seen it fall so I called him for training purposes. He looked at the pheasant, then at me, and decided I could not only see it but that I had hands and he didn't. He went back to hunting. On a hot day he once followed a falling pheasant down into a muddy creek bottom and didn't come back. I went down there and finally found him lying on his belly in four inches of stagnant water. I said he was a bad dog and where was the pheasant? Actually, that is a free translation, as I did not use exactly those words. Kelly stuck his head down and pulled a cock pheasant out from beneath him—at least the muddy mess had the outline of a cock pheasant.

But when he thought I couldn't possibly get to a bird, Kelly performed differently. He followed a falling Alaska ptarmigan over a precipice and came clawing back up with it after I was sure he had been smashed on the rocks below. I put these last stories in to show I am a real world traveler and big-time hunter.

A dog trainer explained things to me.

"The idea is to make the dog want to bring the bird to you. Never go toward him. If he stands there holding it in his mouth, just turn and walk away and he will follow you with the bird and give it to you."

This sounded good and, I could see, was excellent dog psychology. So the next time a big lantern-jawed pointer named Murphy stood and glared at me while holding a bird, I turned and walked in the other direction. After going some distance I peeked back over one shoulder and Murphy had left. I finally found him, but I never saw the bird again.

Retriever men train their Chesapeakes, Labradors and goldens with electric collars. If the dog makes a mistake in practice, he gets zapped. If he isn't paying attention, he gets stung too. A retriever that can't take much of this sort of treatment without turning in his feedpan is washed out and sold to somebody who "just wants to hunt ducks or something."

I went to a retriever field trial and was watching a good Labrador heading off for a complicated series of retrieves when he made a wrong turn. He yelped.

"He knew he was wrong and expected to get shocked," his handler said. "He forgets he isn't wearing the electric collar."

There is still some hope that my dogs will improve their retrieving after I study the subject more. Last winter one brought me a skunk.

Shotgunnery is said to be an art as opposed to the science of rifle marksmanship. I know good shotgunners are possessed because they do not know how they do it and something is guiding them. I am qualified on the subject because I once hit 19 Hungarian partridges straight and missed 19 snipe straight, giving me a cross-section view of the sport.

Chapter Ten

All About Shotgunning

This was a very long time ago and $2,500 was a bundle to spend for a Parker side-by-side with pretty wood, some engraving and a very straight stock.

Monty was not doing too well and since he shot for money he viewed an escaping live pigeon with melancholy. The shoot still had a long way to go and was presenting a dark financial outlook. Monty decided his new Parker was shooting too high, a technical problem to be solved by technical adjustments: the tree limbs had to be exactly the right distance apart.

When the barrels bent downward they parted company with the elevated rib, which left them with a brisk snap. The adjustment completed, Monty did pretty well on the rest of the "fliers" and he was still shooting with what he called the "floating rib" 20-some years later. No use to screw up a winning combination. The rib wouldn't flap until after each shot was fired anyway.

Shotgunnery is said to be an art as opposed to the science of rifle marksmanship. I *know* good shotgunners are possessed because they do not know how they do it and *something* is guiding them. I am qualified on the subject because I once hit 19 Hungarian partridges straight and missed 19 snipe straight, giving me a cross-section view of the sport.

Most American game shots are slow to attend a shooting school or at least pay an expert instructor. This is a result of the popular premise that all Americans are born good shots. Since most of the best shotgunners don't have the slightest idea of what is going on, a deadly grouse or duck shot tends to be the worst consultant available. Asking him how to shoot is like asking Catfish Hunter how to throw a slider and then trying to negotiate a major league contract after he tells you. The best shot I go with asks me every fall which is the more open barrel on his over-under.

I think history shows the level of thinking that surrounds scattergunnery. As recently as the 1920's there were articles in outdoor magazines explaining why it was unnecessary to shoot ahead of flying birds and only some other articles explaining mathematically why that lead was necessary kept such a doctrine from standing. Even today a deadeye grouse banger is likely to tell you that the only way to hit a bird is to shoot right at it, no matter what direction it is headed. Of course he shoots with a built-in swing-through but don't tell him or he may miss from then on. In fact, it is wise to avoid any kind of technical talk near somebody who is killing more than his share of birds.

One of the obstacles in the path of good shotgun shooting is the beauty of various models and the tendency to cling to one that's pretty whether you can shoot it or not. I finally sold the only custom shotgun I ever owned when exhaustive tests proved I could hit better with almost any other gun I owned or could borrow. That took six years, but I am more logical than my friend Luke. That is not his real name.

Luke decided he could afford a really slick custom-built bird gun and when he asked my help in its dimensions I shouldered him aside and grabbed the order blank. I always have known what's best for everybody else.

If the makers had followed my instructions things would have worked out. As it was, the guy who did the stock had ideas of his own; he had an eye for beauty but not for Luke's dimensions. When we rushed to a practice trap with the new gun we found that it had been designed for a very unique shooter, one whose eye was level with his shoulder. Of course straight stocks have a special beauty when the wood is fancy walnut and the sidelock is engraved with everything from lecherous Pans to sensual Dianas.

To hit with Luke's gun we had to point a couple of feet under the target, a bit of physics that became disturbing since you might become intrigued by another part of the landscape and completely forget where or what the target was. Luke talked to his banker and ran down a new stockmaker because the original was on the other side of the ocean.

The new stockmaker used a beautiful piece of walnut, checkered it impeccably and charged enough to pay for an armful of pumpguns. However, he said that the measurements we'd given him made the gun look rather sloppy, so he had used the same ones as for the original.

The last time I went hunting with Luke he was shooting very well indeed. After ten years with it he had become used to the gun and never even had to think about holding two feet low any more. Once I started to suggest Monty's barrel bending with the tree limbs but thought better of it. I think Luke has accepted the fact that holding two feet low is a small price for a really artistic side-by-side.

Although—in theory—a shotgun's measurements are concrete mathematical fact, there are mystic qualities about certain guns that attract or repel shooters, especially hunters, whose success or failure is not accurately measured. Like Luke, some cannot believe a double gun with a thousand dollars worth of engraving and perfect checkering can be less useful than a pitted mail order pump with stovebolts through the cracked stock. Since alteration would reduce the value of a classic, few would consider a little judicial whittling.

My friend Joe found himself at loose ends for a full day in a backwoods sector of the South. He was gunless, the dove season was open and there seemed to be an overpopulation which Joe felt should be remedied. So Joe borrowed a gun from a friendly sharecropper. When it was handed to him, Joe's basic good breeding prevented him from declining.

The barrels had a patina resulting from repeated rustings, the bores were pitted like overused macadam and the once-broken stock was tastefully secured with baling wire. The wood appeared to be weathered scrap from a low-cost housing project. The maker's name had gone the way of abrasion and corrosion but had been cut shallow in the beginning since the maker apparently preferred semi-anonymity.

Once out of sight of the gun's owner, Joe carefully inspected the barrels to make sure they were not black powder Damascus and then forced some shells into the chambers, displacing a small spider. At about that time a pair of doves came whistling past in the direction of a field of milo and Joe, purely out of habit, came up with his picture swing and spilled both of them.

While he extracted the empties with his pocketknife, Joe mused that he might be able to get a mess of birds if he was careful and didn't become too apprehensive of the loose breech (Although I have tried to maintain some suspense, I am aware that by now even a reader who moves his lips could finish the story.) With increasing amazement Joe unfailingly killed doves near and far, regretting that his usual gunning friends could not witness the slaughter.

Much later and back in his distant home, Joe suddenly sat up in bed and realized he probably could have bought the treasure for ten dollars. His Holland & Holland never seemed the same again and Joe quit shooting shortly afterward. He couldn't remember the sharecropper's name and couldn't bring himself to tell his wife he was going to cross the continent to look for a ten-dollar gun.

But you can't tell anyway. Such bargains must be stalked with finesse and carefully feigned boredom. Take the time Phil and I found the 32 Remington on the Indian reservation. We'd just stepped outside a little general store—one of those places where you gradually see that the stock is enormous and varied, even though it looks like junk at first.

"There's a 32 Remington standing in a corner with a bunch of crowbars and shovels," Phil hissed. "I'll offer him 50 bucks after I work around to it."

This was in the late Fifties and the discontinued Remington 32 over-and-under was already being sought diligently by gun nuts. Phil went back into the store and bought some chewing gum and then mentioned that he could see an old shotgun standing over there in the corner. The rustic proprietor handed it to him and just as Phil was about to offer his 50 bucks the old guy yawned, scratched himself and said he didn't think he wanted to sell.

"Feller offered me $1,500 for it last week," he mentioned.

But back to the guns with magic.

Keith came furtively into our house carrying a shotgun as if he had just shoplifted it and was hunting a fence. A gun type who likes pretty ones, he prefers rather costly doubles. The one he was smuggling was a cheap autoloader that had traveled on a fast assembly line. He had tried to make the stock look better and it looked as if someone had tried to make it look better.

"Let's measure this thing!" he said furtively.

I had already guessed his story. He was shooting the auto better than any of his good guns and it made him queasy just to look at it. He'd gotten it for home protection and at first hunted with it just for a brief novelty. We worked out all of the measurements but we had to ignore the occult features which were undoubtedly more important.

There is a strange thing about strange guns, ruefully reported by good trap and skeet shooters. When things aren't going too well it is logical to suspect the gun. The logical thing is to borrow another one and the likely thing is that immediately scores will rise. Gun club psychologists have that all figured out: The shooter's subconscious is sloppily handling his old gun with occasional embarrassing lapses. Then along comes this strange gun and it requires a little more attention so the nervous system snaps to attention and smokes a string of targets, after which the shooter keeps his old car and buys the borrowed winner. A few targets later the subconscious relaxes and he's back where he started, only the new gun may not be quite as good as old Betsy. This phenomenon delights the builders of gun cabinets, some models of which cover entire walls.

Anyone having trouble with his shooting can usually find helpful advice but should beware of those who call out his shots for him. For example, if an observer tells him repeatedly that he is shooting high at practice targets, even though he points lower each time, he should run a little experiment and fire into the ground immediately below the target. If the observer calls out, "High again!" his coach's credibility is in question.

There are a great many experienced coaches who can see the shot in the air (it looks like an out-of-focus swarm of gnats) and quite a few less-experienced coaches who say they can but they can't. We all have our pride.

Shotgunners hardly ever confess to buck fever but their nervous systems produce something remarkably like it. I am reminded of Paul, the fine skeet shooter, who, nevertheless, had never broken 100 straight. It became known around the club that as the magic number was approached Paul tended to take off the pressure by missing a target by three or four feet.

Came the day when he seemed to be on the way, the clays disappearing in little puffs as he approached the final stations with what appeared to be complete confidence. Tragedy struck at Station Six where he swung on a target and heard only a click. It developed that Paul had loaded a cigaret instead of a cartridge.

But then, Alice was crossing a fence in South Carolina when she noted a pair of rigid pointers just ahead and hurried a little with her reloading, then attempted to drop a quail with her 20-gauge lipstick in her L. C. Smith.

First-timers at plantation quail gunning with shooting wagons and mules behind mounted dog handlers are understandably shaken at first at the formality of the situation when someone calls, "Point!" and he is handed his shotgun by a guy with a flushing whip. I will not even use a fictitious name for the poor soul who scored a double on mules after one of them sneezed.

Types of shotgun actions have furnished fuel for argument and the British have taken this very seriously indeed for the past 75 or 80 years. Generations of new Englishmen have come on with new argument on the old subject.

The traditional shotgun, of course, is a side-by-side double and I am surprised that the British have not had other types legally banned. And although trap and skeet shooters now view side-by-side as a novelty, the British can stand there in their tweeds and slap down driven grouse with discouraging consistency, using side-by-sides. Some of them insist on calling those upstart guns *under-and-overs* instead of *over-and-unders*, the only thing I really resent about English shotgunnery. The British make photos showing how a double (no elevated rib) gives a better view of the target under various light conditions.

Of course "repeaters," whether pump or auto, have never been accepted in the upper crust of British shooting, even if they bear an engraved image of the Crown. At first, the impression is that repeater pointing is associated with game hoggery, but using a skilled loader to hand him another gun as needed, a top hand can shoot faster than anybody could with an autoloader over the long haul. He *never* has to stop to reload.

There is a romantic notion today that virtually all of the old market hunters used double guns. That they did until things like the 1897 Winchester pump came along, whereupon most of the more serious commercial types set their old doubles in the corner. Then when the autoloaders began to stop jamming they, too, got a big piece of the action.

Despite the proven fact that in modern shotguns the velocity difference between a 24-inch barrel and a 40-inch barrel is barely measurable and certainly never noticed by any species of bird, there is still sale for goose probers with snouts difficult to conceal in a blind. It has long been known that shotgunners would rather not be confused by facts.

Some who shoot successfully for money are a bit set in their ways and it is difficult to dispute a fellow's habits when he goes home with new silverware each weekend. One of those guys had a special rack built in the engine compartment of his Cadillac and kept his trapshooting ammunition there, explaining that a little heat increased the potency of his shells.

Efforts at mechanical aids for shotgun pointing have hardly ever been dramatically successful. There were things like the optical device that showed the place to point, the low-powered telescopic sight, the tube device that placed a colored dot where the shot would go and the elevated rib. Only the elevated rib has proved its worth for experienced shooters and only a few years back a champion skeet shooter said he did better without it—for a few rounds. The obvious conclusion is that he was going through the "new-gun" phase that causes temporary marksmanship and I am sure he's back to the ventilated ribs by now.

Completely logical but of limited value were the "sighting arms" attached to rifles during World War II. The idea (it had been tried before that, I understand) was that by unfolding some little arms bearing front sights you could shoot the right distance ahead of an enemy airplane. However, rifle fire from the ground has never been a major hazard for aircraft. Evidently hitting an airplane with a rifle bullet is much harder than it looks and such things mounted on shotguns haven't led to new game laws. Besides, they catch in the brush.

Although they still haven't produced a mechanical aid to the nervous system I think today's shooter may be better than the old timers. Legendary tales of the 19th century market hunters and competition shooters of that time have lost little in long repetition but the common remark that "you can shoot at all the clay targets you want to but no game shooter can get as much practice as the old timers," is no longer valid.

For a price, an American gunner can travel to Central or South America and wear out his gun on endless flocks of doves. I doubt if even Adam Bogardus or Dr. Carver killed more than 200 birds a day very often.

But that doesn't make it a science.

No, Jack had never seen Duchess work, but the man had said (oh, brother!) that she was a nice dog but that he had to move to another town and couldn't take her along. Then Jack broke up about the interview with Duchess' former owner. Jack had asked what training she had and the man said that Jack didn't understand. This was a bird dog, he said, (not a trick dog) and didn't need training.

Chapter Eleven

Any Way, You Pay

No matter how you go about getting one, top-notch bird dogs are all about the same price.

This is a favorite line of mine and I'm going to explain it and stand by it, but my rule can be suspended by sheer luck. There have been pointing poodles and retrieving Airedales, so I'm talking about averages you can count on. There are dogs like the Duchess of Doonesbury, whom I'll tell you about and who riddle my theory, but there are many more who average it out.

The theory is that you can keep trying pups, spending two or three years on each one, until you get a hotshot. Pups don't usually start out very expensive, even from good stock, but by the time you've been with one of them for the three years usually demanded for finishing you've put in a lot of time, bought a lot of dog food, paid for a lot of shots and probably anted up for some other veterinarian's bills. At the end of those three years you have a buddy you probably can't part with, but it's likely you won't have a top-notch bird dog, in which case you'd better start over again if pups are your way to go.

Or you can start getting inexpensive adult dogs of the chosen breed. You can pick them up from newspaper or magazine ads; you can get them from dog pounds; or you can go to dog dealers and ask for cheapies in the pointing breeds. Eventually you'll land a sleeper like the Duchess of Doonesbury, but you'll probably spend a lot of cash before it happens. All this is quicker than the pup business but just as expensive.

Or you can buy a finished dog of three years or so—a dog you might be able to try out before writing a check, and one that "does it all" as the dog men say. That includes good bird finding, staunch pointing and retrieving and careful dead hunting, a badly neglected phase of the business.

So it all costs about the same. The toughest part is discarding the failures, especially the captivating pup that has become a part of the family. Better just keep him as a pet. About 90 per cent of the bird hunters are running second-rate or third-rate dogs that they won't give up. They keep telling themselves (and you) that old Sport is a whiz, even if he can't find his own dish on a clear day.

The Duchess of Doonesbury is a partnership dog, and although I have tried to buy Jack out, he won't consider it. The Duchess cost $100 (with her doghouse included) but I think Jack could have gotten her for $50. He got her at the end of last season. Fool luck. Well, not completely fool luck since Jack knows what an English pointer should look like, but he bought Duchess as a long shot. Jack will do that kind of thing now and then.

He called me from clear across the country. Seems he had this two-year-old lady pointer he'd met in Idaho and he had no place to keep her. Would I go partners and help him handle her? Hadn't cost much, and if she didn't know a quail from a mongoose we could get rid of her. I don't trust dogs named things like Duchess but Jack is a super-salesman. I was hooked before I had the fine print sorted out.

No, Jack had never seen Duchess work, but the man had said (oh, brother!) that she was a nice dog but that he had to move to another town and couldn't take her along. Then Jack broke up about the interview with Duchess' former owner. Jack had asked what training she had and the man said that Jack didn't understand. This was a bird dog, he said, (not a trick dog) and didn't *need* training.

"You see," the man explained patiently, "when she smells these birds she points at them and then when you shoot them she brings them to you. No training."

He could tell Jack was pretty stupid, I guess, thinking that you had to train a bird dog and all. In the case of Duchess the man was right, but I can't help thinking of the surprises he'll be in for when he starts out with some other dog.

Duchess (we shortened it to Dutch) didn't know her name, but she learned it in about 20 minutes. The first time she was put down she went over the horizon, and since she didn't know about whistles and loud yells, we put an electric collar on her. Dutch would come in looking hurt. Why didn't we explain it if we wanted her in closer? No more trouble with that.

Dutch weighs 55 pounds and is mostly steel springs and jet fuel. Since she didn't know a dog crate from a steamer trunk, I said, "Kennel up!" and she slithered in like an eel on her own, even if the door was a little small. Needn't get rough about it. Just say what you want.

You know the rest of it. When she found the birds she froze. The only problem in retrieving was which shooter to bring them to so she decided to divide them up as fairly as possible. We took her chukar hunting and found she could mark a gliding cripple so far away it was only a speck. She'd get it and bring it back up the mountain.

I guess Dutch really didn't need training. I have not asked her to shoot or cook birds, but I suspect it could be worked out. I wish Jack would sell his part. I have her here in Florida and if something happens to her, he'll put out a contract on me. Jack lives in Montana.

Despite the morbid thoughts of classic bird-dog men who say no dog can handle mature Huns, much of my pleasure and agony is in association with long-time canine Hun hunters. Most are perpetually confused and surprised at where the birds really are. A few become schemers and conspirators who eye you like owl-hooters planning a bank job when they get a sniff of Hun. I have known a couple who grinned from ear to ear and began to tippy-toe at the slightest whiff of grey partridge.

Chapter Twelve

Greying Hunters Hunting Greys

"**G**rey partridge" is a better name but I've always called them "Huns," from *Hungarian*. I prefer not to think of them as *Hunkies*.

They came to America from central Europe, largely from Hungary, I understand. An exotic gamebird in conservative dress, settling quietly in a new hemisphere and adapting to new conditions.

Back in Europe the beaters drive them to aristocratic gunners, and there have been times when I needed a few beaters myself. When some American biologists were doing a study on them a few years back (a long-neglected project and badly needed) I approached a project leader for the latest dope. The personnel and scientific gadgets were ready for use, he said.

"Now if we can just catch some of the damned things!" he snapped.

By devious methods I obtained a copy of a biologist's report which covered the attempts at catching adult Huns for scientific purposes. In straight-faced biologist's language it was hilarious, especially the part about the Oriental mist net (a fine-stranded net supposed to be unnoticed by birds until they flew into it). The Huns went under, over and around the net, even when it was trolled by speeding jeeps.

The relocation of the Hun to the United States is a mystery story, so vaguely documented that I have even resorted to some of my own works of past years. It seems that the earliest serious attempts to establish the bird in this hemisphere were made around 1900 in Washington, Oregon and Alberta; but Americans being what they are, I suppose a few birds had been uncrated almost anywhere there was a faint chance of survival.

Early attempts in the eastern farmlands weren't particularly successful, although a distribution map will show pockets of them all across the northern states. It appears that the best foothold was gained in Alberta—and those birds (we think) have populated our northwestern states, where they live around grainfields as well as on high grasslands and mountain slopes that Huns aren't supposed to like but sometimes do.

I like a quote from Dan Holland, who wrote *The Upland Game Hunter's Bible,* a paperback of 1961 which deserves more attention than it gets. Holland says:

"Apparently these birds OF A 1906 PLANTING IN WASHING-TON WHEATFIELDS EAST OF THE CASCADES didn't know they had ever left home. They filled their crops with grain, settled down to a life of ease and plenty, raised healthy children and discussed plans for thwarting the Hungarian beaters which they expected during the coming autumn drives."

Ben Williams of Montana may be America's leading Hun hunter. But don't get excited, Ben. You don't have much competition because the Hun has no tradition, glamour or press agent—except me, and I don't work at it full time.

Ben, a sort of boondock track star, once followed a covey of Huns through nine successive flushes. Or was it 11? Anyway, that kind of Hun hunting is athletic. Ben has a constant hunting companion, an eager beaver named Dr. John Cey. The idea is that these guys hunt in some of Montana's high grassland with a corps of Brittanies. They keep chasing the birds, either seeing them land after a flush or guessing where they'll be. After Huns land they tend to run. I am not referring to bobwhite trotting. I mean *run*. Getting a lot of flushes from the same covey doesn't necessarily mean a lot of birds. On some days, especially windy and snowy ones, they tend to get up wild, and several flushes don't necessarily mean that many shots, or even any shot at all.

The most flushes I got from a single covey before it broke apart was five, and the fifth was from exactly the same spot I jumped them the first time. A well-organized bunch is likely to follow a fairly rigid flush-and-land schedule, using the same spots and ending up where they started. They don't always. Often the last lap is done on foot, up to several hundred yards. If your pointer comes in and looks up at you with a harried expression, be sympathetic. After all, a dog can feel insecure when pointing is measured by the mile.

Since the European birds were primarily grain-eaters and since wheat, rye, barley and the like are preferred habitat in this country, there are gunners who call in their dogs when they run out of cereals. But in a good year the Huns scatter to chukar habitat. I have found sassy coveys at 8,000 feet on a rocky slope where I was panting after mule deer in the patchy snow. There was no grain near that spot. Like the chukar, the Hun can be comfortable in cheat grass.

Some of Ben Williams' most reliable hunting is high pasture country he has worked for some 15 years, and those birds don't have grain. I have one place of my own, a series of rocky sagebrush knobs with water nearby (urgent requirement) where I have found birds for a decade. The productive area is only a half mile across, mostly up and down, and the birds buzz around those knobs as long as you will chase them, although they will get harder and harder to locate as the day wears on and the coveys scatter. Some years back Ed Gray was up there, and as we were getting ready to leave he looked off across a hundred square miles of such knobs and marvelled at the number of Huns there must be. Forget it, Ed. I wore out a set of Vibram soles on those other hills. The birds are on those three little humps.

A man told me of coming upon a covey of Huns playing on a hillside. The snow was just right, and he said they were taking turns going down a slide on their rumps. I don't think I believe that.

One November I was hunting a steep slope with only a single patch of snow about 20 feet across. A large and fat covey of Huns was sitting in that snow and the patch was trampled and splotched with droppings, indicating they had been living there while there was plenty of sun-warmed grass over the rest of the hill. I asked some biologists about this but they immediately clammed up, looked suspicious and wouldn't even explain the things they *did* understand, so I don't say much about the snow-patch Huns.

They're especially hard to hunt in snow, generally being pretty wild and unwilling to hold for a dog. When they feed in the snow their heads appear briefly as tiny black dots as they peer around before going back to the foraging for seeds. Marcus Crosby, an addicted Hun watcher, sat on a ridge last fall with binoculars and pointed out Hun coveys to me—little dark areas that kept changing shapes far down there on the white field. As they plowed about in the snow the birds were sometimes completely concealed.

Good eyes, and I mean really good eyes, are a great help with the high-country Huns, the ones that live on the sweeping flats and the brushy draws just below the rimrock. I am about 20 years past the efficiency point in that business.

The dog points and moves and points a few more times and I puff along behind him, knowing that when the birds go they will probably be pretty well out. If he'd been steady the first time he stopped, there might have been one of those treasured moments when the birds hold like bobwhite quail and go cheeping up around your ears. But if they're running, there's no telling. My version of scientific accounting has shown the average rise from which a bird is killed to be about 15 yards—which translates into a 35-yard shot most of the time, unless you're the fastest gun in the West.

When they go up, whether I get a shot or not, I try to mark them down. It looks easy at first but they tend to sweep in a great curve, alternately silhouetted against the sky and unseen against the grey sagebrush and the brown grass of late fall. Then things get a little confused and the cluster of dots somehow merges with the little dark specks permanently installed in my retinas (the doctor calls them "floaters"). Generally they just fly out of sight unless I can get my binoculars on them. The latter is not as easy as it sounds if I've shot a bird and tried to mark it down, or have missed and paused to swear or scream at the dog. Half the time I am so spooked I forget my glasses anyway. I simply trudge off in the general direction they flew.

Despite the morbid thoughts of classic bird-dog men who say no dog can handle mature Huns, much of my pleasure and agony is in association with long-time canine Hun hunters. Most are perpetually confused and surprised at where the birds really are. A few become schemers and conspirators who eye you like owl-hooters planning a bank job when they get a sniff of Hun. I have known a couple who grinned from ear to ear and began to tippy-toe at the slightest whiff of grey partridge.

If there is such a thing as a typical Hun debacle, I guess it happened last fall on the knobs where my old Brittany, Tex, an individual noted for enthusiasm if not staunchness or style, froze with his stub tail vibrating and his breath coming jerkily. It was a miniature swale on a steep hillside that dropped off into a draw with near vertical sides. I had first found Huns in that spot during the Johnson administration. I walked in from the side so old Tex could see me and wouldn't get worried. Walked in well ahead of him so I'd be that much closer to the birds that would go up 15 yards from his nose. But there was no spatter of wings or avian squeals of dismay. It's common enough for a cautious Hun dog to point when the birds are too far off so I walked cautiously in the direction Tex was headed. I'd gone too far, I decided, and turned back toward Tex, now locked in a hypnotic stare as if the birds were under his nose. As I started to walk back toward him the Huns went up behind me, a full-fledged clatter-and-squeak flush—still a good way off but within satisfactory range. Twenty yards?

Aha! I pivoted with my gun coming up as smoothly as a gun can come up for me when it is to be pointed in the direction I've just come from. Flash of grey-and-tan birds roaring down toward the draw proper and time to shoot. That was when the other birds went up back under Tex's nose where I'd walked past them.

With the cool logic I display at such times I concluded it would be easier to shoot the birds near Tex so I abandoned my gesture toward the others and stabbed at the four headed over the ridge. I fired so efficiently my shots almost rolled together in a single report, as they used to say of the Western gunfighters. Not even a feather fell and with an empty gun I watched the things go squeaking and buzzing over the rocky top. I have no recollection of where my muzzle was pointed.

Then, for the first time in our long association, Tex really forgot himself. He stood and barked at me. The stinking potlicker.

The most humiliating thing about Huns as targets is their wide range of speeds. When a big covey takes off at close range it may go pretty well up before choosing a direction, or they might flap out like so many overweight bantams. Take a nice, open twenty gauge and poke at them. Blap! Blap! Fetch!

The next time they buzz instead of flap, leave from 25 yards away and have broken the sound barrier before they're five feet in the air. It is too late to go back for the full-choke duck gun. But if you had it, you would probably have one of those shirt-button rises where you can feel the wind on your face.

Ben Williams uses an over-under twenty, improved and modified. Cey uses a side-by-side, same boring. Since Huns are in the open, why not always use a tightly bored gun? No reason except that there's some kind of mental hazard, I think. Seven-and-a-half shot is about right unless you are a full-choke pointer, when sixes might be a good choice.

They say Huns can ruin a good dog. My white setter Danny wasn't getting any full-page stories in *The American Field* to begin with, but I believe he really became a degenerate the evening we hunted those draws above Tom Lane's wheat-fields. It was early season and for some reason the Huns were holding a picnic at the edge of some stubble. As nearly as I can figure there were seven coveys there and they flew in all directions. Danny pointed in all directions, the Hun scent evidently hanging in the September air like warm smog. When I picked up Danny and several Huns he had a funny look in his eyes. It was a month before he pointed again.

These Hun gatherings are not unusual, but I don't understand them. The typical complete Hun covey of early season is a family group with a dozen to 16 birds. This covey has its own escape plan. When it joins other birds to make up a big flock it keeps its strategy on file. Flush the big bunch in a single, ragged uprising and each covey will head for its own hideout. That's what Ben Williams says. I had supposed they just split up at random but I can see it now.

I know where Huns rest at midday. They want enough vegetation for concealment but they want it open enough to run in and to take off from without too much wing battering. They also want to watch you as you slink up the draw. Only a very young, tired or confused Hun dives into really thick brush.

There are some Hun rules, and while frequently suspended, they give you a good start. Like the quail expert who marked a scattered bunch of bobwhites into a hollow and then showed me he could kick up four to my one without a dog, there are Hun hunters who have a feeling for where the birds go and stop.

There's the business about walking over a hill. When a covey alights on the near side of a rise the chances are they'll walk out of sight over the top before settling down. Follow them over the crest and then get your finger next to the safety.

But it's the reversal that keeps me from getting cocky. I have watched a full covey sail into an arroyo from a field of sage and followed them confidently, only to find the dog acting a little retarded instead of pointing where I was sure they should be. Then, walking back the way I'd come, I've found they'd actually hiked back past me, my hunting buddy and the dog and were back where they'd started, although somewhat scattered. I considered giving the dog a nasal spray.

Certain conditions make them fly faster. I have never understood why Huns fly faster when they're in rocky canyons, but some of the rimrock whistlers have cost me considerable ammunition. There have been occasions when the same birds got a little confused and passed me several times. Of course, standing on a near-vertical canyon wall is not conducive to the best marksmanship and provides a ready-made alibi. However, if I were standing on flat concrete with my gun mounted and could yell, "Pull," I'd still miss most of them. Chukars, bonefish and Huns suspend my mental machinery.

The best Hun dogs are likely to display varied tactics. Although some of the good ones run hard and stop quick in the time-honored style admired by quail hunters, there are days when Huns won't freeze but will take off while the dog is still legging it, certain he isn't yet close enough to point.

I confess that the best Hun dog I have ever seen was what I call cautious and what dog experts call piddling. He became a gumshoer at the first whiff of Hun, made most of his points from considerable distance and generally moved the last 30 yards on tiptoe. This has obvious advantages when you're hunting wild flushers because you can hurry up and be with the dog as he closes in. Not exactly classic form, but a hell of a good way to kill a Hun or two.

I would like to get poetic about Huns for nobody else has. I like them in Oregon dry country when they flush from the edge of a giant erosion and swerve with the air currents caused by a ribbon of river far below. It is wonderful in Alberta when they leave the stubble and go against a backdrop of blue sky and a bright orange grain elevator. In Montana they flush from the abandoned homestead where they and their ancestors have lived half a century.

I love to look for them in the edges of the golden stubble, but perhaps the high-grassland Huns are best of all. The country is wilder and more lonely. Small European gamebirds making a home where the summers are dry and the winters are cold.

Scatter the covey and look fruitlessly for it as night comes on, your dog confused by occasional shreds of scent, finding nothing. Bone-tired, unload your gun and start back toward the truck as true night closes in. There's an occasional bullbat when the first stars show and a little wind in the grass. Then you hear the faint, reedy sound somewhere on the shadowy slope. A lonely Hun asking about his friends.

I am not sure that I really want people to read what I write about dying dogs and I have written in detail about them very few times.

Chapter Thirteen

The Barrier

Dog people are sentimentalists and when we write about dogs we eventually come to the sad parts, and sometimes we fill them in awkwardly, the death of a hunting dog sometimes recorded in such agonizing sorrow that the reader recoils from it. A writer may go farther than he would with the loss of a human friend and when I write about a dog's death I have a fear that it is mawkish and that some reader will curl his lip and say, "Boy, he sure pulled out all the stops on that one."

I am not sure that I really want people to read what I write about dying dogs and I have written in detail about them very few times. But I can understand what it is about a dog's death that makes it so poignant. It is that however close an owner is to a dog there is the fact that he and the dog, whatever he may say, can never communicate as two people can and he always wonders if the dog really understands. It may be that the dog, with a simple worship for his master, doesn't want to understand more than he does. But after looking into a great many questioning canine eyes I am afraid they spend much of their lives trying to understand things they cannot. The barrier.

And when a hunting dog dies, especially if you had him "put down" as we say when a veterinarian ends his life mercifully, you wonder if he understood that you once punished him for his own good to keep him from running out into traffic. You wonder if the painless ending is welcomed by the dog who thus avoids lingering suffering, and my wife, who understands dogs better than I do, has stroked their heads while they received fatal injections.

Those times you may have gotten a little too harsh in training come before you from time to time when a dog dies but I do not doubt that most of them have been long forgotten by the dog. Again, we have the barrier that can never be broken. These feelings, I believe, are stronger when the dog has spent much of its time in your house and has traveled with you. I do not want to agonize long over these things but I cannot forget the beginning of them for me—the first dog that was really all mine and strangely, probably the most intelligent dog I ever owned. He was apart from other farm dogs. It was a long time ago.

The farm was on a dirt road in Kansas and five miles from a small town. I suppose it was someone "from town" who dumped unwanted pups along Cow Creek. There were two and a neighbor boy appropriated one, the one that seemed most desirable at the time. Mine was longer-haired, leggier, and largely English setter, although I did not know it then. In fact, I had never seen a dog point, despite the coveys of bobwhites along the creek.

Addicted to western novels which I had begun to read at a ridiculously tender age, I named my dog Ranger, which didn't seem theatrical at all at the time. I hunted rabbits with him (he would point part of the time) and he was a constant companion and a self-appointed guardian although I didn't realize that part until I splashed a little while dog-paddling in the north farm pond. I came out of that with numerous abrasions, for when a dog tries to drag what he thinks is a drowning kid from the water he can't be too careful about how he clamps his teeth. I will not go on with Ranger's untrained brilliance for this is about his death, but we were inseparable for some years. Ranger was terribly injured when my father and I accidentally dropped a cypress rowboat on him when unloading it from a makeshift trailer—the running gears of an old buggy.

It was a spinal injury which no veterinarian could have helped and he was partly paralyzed. It was unusual for the veterinarian to even look at a farm dog in those days but my father did have Ranger checked and confirmed there was no chance of recovery—only a life of suffering. "Put down" was not a phrase I remember from those days but my father said Ranger must be shot and that I would have to do it.

I do not know if he intended to build my character or if my father was simply too tender-hearted in this case to do the shooting himself. It was several days before I could handle it and I kept stopping Ranger from crawling off into the bushes to die, knowing what he was trying to do.

Anyway, it was winter time and Ranger slept in the sun. I hid behind something in the farmyard, waited until he dozed off in the granary doorway and killed him instantly from some distance with a .22 bullet from my rifle, using a rest.

I do not think it built my character but it brought me a strange sense of command of the entire situation. I did not want to talk about it and I would bury the dog myself. It was no one else's business. I took Ranger to a little hillside and buried him as I have buried other dogs since and no one else knew where the grave was. I did not want a marker. Any marker. The grave was private, to stay private. More than half a century has passed and the steep little hillside has overgrown with brush and some good-sized elms, but I know where the grave is. I can take you there.

Crawling sweatily through a dry wash toward a herd
of antelope I had stalked for almost two hours, I saw
my first sage grouse, apparently either a seven-pound
quail or the product of a rebelling nervous system. I
was crawling on a plane with jackrabbit droppings
and an occasional dried bone of indeterminate origin,
and he seemed to tower above me as he stood with
upstretched neck. When I described him as a seven-
pound quail an editor deleted it with no stated reason.
I submit the comparison again as a sort of test.

Chapter Fourteen

Shadows on the Prairie

The largest grouse—the sage hen—must have sage, and sage depends upon the price of wheat, the need for coal and the living space that man demands.

Before the buffalo and the cattle grubbed down the tides of grass, the sage existed mainly on only the higher ground. But the shrub spread its range where the grass gave way and some of the grass eaters changed their life styles. The pronghorn was one. But the sage hen seems always to have favored the sage brush.

Because of its sameness the sage seems endless, and where it still stands man has left little mark. The double trails of rattling pickup trucks are not much different from those of creaking wagons with grunting oxen and the landscape of brush and towering sky seems even more lonely when it is broken by the tiny cipher of a monument. "Sheepherders' monuments," we say, although any lonely man on any timeless mission could have built one—a little tower of stones that was likely to be the most permanent mark he would leave upon the world—to last longer and to be seen more often than his gravestone, if he was to have one.

I think of sage hens and "monuments" together as I think of sage hens and prairie-dog towns, distant antelope and drifting coyotes, turning golden eagles and the sandhill cranes going south. And although it can be that way, I find it hard to remember sage hens flailing at sage and rabbit brush at my feet in a touch-and-go duel with gravity—the procedure that causes better gunners to say this is no game bird.

I think of sage hens as moving shadows a quarter mile ahead on stony ground that has kept the sage thin. I know they are watching me and probably will not wait, and I can remember them flying higher and higher to set their wings briefly and choose a course, whereupon I always say exactly the same thing:

"They're leaving the country."

And there is the little bunch at great height, flying against a chilling backdrop of snow-promising sky and over a white spine of the Rockies toward some winter range I do not know.

When the history books first spoke of the "prairie chicken" they undoubtedly meant sage hens part of the time, but after Lewis and Clark met the grizzled, hump-backed bear they were not likely to go deeply into the taxonomy of plains birdlife. And the mountain men and then the settlers who came afterward saw the plains' birds as essential though sometimes infrequent meals. Some were simply larger than others.

Then there were graceful rifles that came from Pennsylvania by way of Kentucky, and there were a few sleek fowling pieces; but it is likely that more of the sage grouse fell to nondescript guns remade from muskets of the Revolution, and few birds were shot in flight. When man is a stranger, sage hens are fools.

Only a few years ago the sage hens became so scarce that it seemed hunting them was gone forever, but then they came back to open seasons over much of the West. The farthest north I have killed a sage hen was in southern Alberta.

The danger now is the immense articulated diesel tractor that can rip up sage-covered land the pioneer's sod plow could not turn. That will depend upon how beef and wheat profits compare and how the cattleman judges the use of chemicals for pastureland. Sage grouse are primarily leaf eaters, although their rather flimsy gizzards may contain some grain. And while they may search for green shoots in stubble fields and love alfalfa, the sage is never far away.

Few know sage grouse except from the pictures taken or painted during the grouse's big scene in early spring as the snows are going and the cocks gather at their strutting grounds in displays only the wild turkey can rival, but only because he is larger. Indian costumes for ceremonial dances were made more in imitation of the sage grouse than of the eagle. Except for the mating ritual the bird merges with the sage and excites no magazine covers.

Crawling sweatily through a dry wash toward a herd of antelope I had stalked for almost two hours, I saw my first sage grouse, apparently either a seven-pound quail or the product of a rebelling nervous system. I was crawling on a plane with jackrabbit droppings and an occasional dried bone of indeterminate origin, and he seemed to tower above me as he stood with upstretched neck. When I described him as a seven-pound quail an editor deleted it with no stated reason. I submit the comparison again as a sort of test.

Like gunners who assign a certain speed to each game bird and do not concede he can go faster or slower, casual observers of sage grouse make factual pronouncements that startle more careful students.

A sage hen will sometimes stand and watch a hunter's approach with no effort at concealment, leading to the instant conclusion that he can neither hide nor run, but he does both very well.

Bobwhite quail that move 200 yards under the frustrated supervision of pointers are called "running birds." A bunch of sage grouse will go just faster than a man's walk for two miles—and when a hunter or his dog finally gets too close it may be that only one or two birds go up, the rest having disappeared in cover somewhere along the route. But you may hunt sage hens for years without such an exhibition.

There are times when birds of the year will make a foolish attempt at concealment in close-cropped grass several feet from the sage, but the adults hide well when they try, and a hunter sometimes brushes a five-pound bird with his foot before it batters its way into the air, a disconcerting experience that sometimes results in ridiculous shooting displays. Remember that in early season there may be alert rattlesnakes in sage grouse range.

The giants are the cocks, perhaps even seven pounds, while the hens are more likely to weigh a little more than two. When they walk, the cocks have a tendency to waddle; the hens walk evenly, their feet apparently put down with deliberate caution. But in the air the hens execute a violent twist at intervals as if one wing might have failed momentarily—and when it occurs as a shot is missed the gunner is likely to feel he has a hard cripple. This twist-in-flight appears not only in escape. I have watched it in birds flying so high that I might not have identified them otherwise.

To most gunners the sage grouse is an incidental bird to be pursued only the first day or two of the season, and the methods used are hardly aesthetic. A row of shooters in skirmish order will kill sage grouse, especially early in the fall, and the score is aided if they have a flushing dog or two. Birds of the spring hatch make mistakes in the direction of flight they choose.

Where early-season birds are fairly plentiful and the sage spotty, binoculars work for hunters who simply park a truck and scan surrounding hills. If the birds move about, they can be seen, slow-moving dark spots against sun-cooked grass; but if they are resting, a long inspection reveals nothing but possibly a drifting coyote or antelope or a searching hawk.

There are formulae, however, for resting sage grouse. In typical sage habitat they are most likely to be in the draws— where the sage is heaviest and not far from water; and if the water's edge is muddy, their big tracks are a sure thing in an uncertain business. Then, of course, there are the droppings to look for, subjects of endless argument, for no one knows just how long sage-hen droppings will survive the seasons. A year? Two?

The shredding grey ones, widely scattered, mean simply that a sage hen (possibly long dead) has walked that way. If there is some green and black in the droppings, they are fairly recent. If they are clustered in piles, the birds have rested there, each leaving his own collection. And "caecal droppings," black liquid that hardens in temporary blots on the ground, mean fairly recent bird presence.

Last fall we went to new sage country and we were late. The first shooters had driven the Bureau of Land Management roads in eastern Montana, and here and there the sun glanced off empty shotgun shells in or near the trail. Several times we found scattered feathers where someone had dressed his kill. It was warm and dry despite our lateness, and more than a mile away a film of dust rose over someone's cattle herd being relocated for the late fall. Dust swirled inside our truck, too. But dry weather can be a help, for although it may be that sage hens can live on dew, they will try to stay near water.

We came to a classic spot, a valley with heavier sage along the nearly dry creek, bare shoulders on some of the slopes and little grooves with thicker sage and rabbit brush near the ridge crests. On the ground was scattered winterfat, the earth-hugging little plant sage grouse are supposed to favor when the northers drive buckshot snow across the flats. There were no really high hills, just several knobs with their miniature walls of rimrock, and some irregular white dots near the horizon instantly translated into a band of antelope who had watched us since we first entered the basin. And to make us feel at home, there was a solitary herder's monument, like an overweight fencepost on top of the highest hill.

I put down the dog, an orange and white Brittany with more steam than judgment, and I watched him tear up along the nearly dry creek. An orange and white dog is discord in purple sage, an interloper where canines should be grey and ghostly.

I found fresh sign within a hundred yards and watched my emissary hopefully as he left the bottom and swept the slopes, one slithering stop and stylish point crumbling to embarrassment as a lazy jackrabbit loafed off ahead of him, loping sidewise. On some days the dog might have chased with urgent yips, but this time he pretended not to notice.

The basin bent to the right and the dog came back to heavier brush near the bottom and was out of sight. Then part way up the slope he reappeared to point so far ahead of me that I despaired of getting there in time. Fidgety dogs do not display their staunchest qualities when large birds stroll about them like field-trial judges assessing form.

Several birds went up in a scatter—bulky forms skimming the sage at first and then towering slightly to spread out and soar over the hilltop. The dog, evidently feeling his primary mission had been accomplished and that it was now time for a bit of relaxation, then methodically put up a dozen more, one at a time, while I screamed helplessly.

But by then I was within a hundred yards of him and he eyed me with some apprehension, loped off to one side and pointed rigidly. When I was still 20 yards behind him a sage hen went up ten yards ahead of him and I killed that bird. Then the same thing happened again, after which came a humiliating miss with both barrels.

We turned back toward the truck, for some of the birds had gone that way, and I cut across a hill to shorten the trip and, as usual, was amazed to see that the truck was only a blue speck. Until then my legs had not seemed tired. Now I was thirsty and even contemplated the grimy canteen I had brought for the dog.

Back at the truck the panting Brittany circled a little and pointed scarcely 50 yards behind it. Then we were really in sage grouse and they went up all around me, all seeming to eye me as they chose escape routes. I killed the third and final bird of my limit and wondered how so many had moved into the area. I investigated the sign and recalled the direction my dog had gone when he first struck the ground. He had simply missed them, and a dozen limits of sage grouse had been there all the time while I had tramped miles of sage.

There are, of course, perfect places for sage grouse that never seem to hold them, and other areas that seem no different from a hundred surrounding square miles but that have had sage grouse for the 20 years I have hunted them. There is one such place, a little island of sage brush half a mile distant from thousands of acres of solid growth. The little island of brush sits in grassland, and there a little bunch of sage hens has been for 20 years, possibly a hundred years for all I know. Perhaps some of them were part of the winter meat for the homesteader whose cabin slowly crumbles in dry wind beneath the ridge a mile away.

It is the fall and winter concentrations that most confuse sage-hen hunters, and an area that has been hard hunted with scanty result at the season's beginning may suddenly be alive with birds at some later date. It happened to me in good antelope country when I came back to a sage-grouse hunting spot as the pronghorn season opened. There was spitting snow where the sun had broiled me and a pair of huffing dogs a month before. And there were several hundred acres of sage grouse, seemingly spaced for the hunter's convenience and going up with predictable regularity. I assume they had moved in for the winter but the location of such a rendezvous is not always the same.

And such a concentration is not necessarily hunter's heaven. Last year, confidently hunting country where I had killed early-season grouse without much difficulty, I found the area seemed suddenly deserted. There was probably six square miles of it with all the sage-hen necessities, including two herder's monuments and the remains of a weathered homestead.

We had hunted all day without sight of a sage grouse and the ones we finally saw went up wild. Wild for the dog who could not hold them and very wild for us, the flushing birds gathering others as they went until there were a hundred against the evening sky and they became specks and disappeared with no sign of alighting. And this time there were no sleepers, no sluggards to wait us out and croak up under our guns. All of them were together and all of them had gone.

When roosting, sage grouse tend to stay fairly close together, but the average flock put up in daytime will be spread out, perhaps over 50 acres or more and scattered so thinly that I cannot say how they get together again. The "sleeper" is the bird most frequently bagged and he is nearly always there if the flock is big. Perhaps he may move hardly at all in the 12 hours after the main flock leaves, and many times I have returned after a long hunt to try once more where I had previously given up, and found one or two birds still there. Of course, occasionally they have returned after flushing earlier in the day, this being a rendezvous point.

But it is his home that lures me after the sage grouse—a country scorned by sightseers and called simply "empty" by passersby with their eyes on distant peaks or singing forests of pine.

There was the trip with Charles Eustace in eastern Montana. A game biologist, his job was to catalog the sage-grouse population, and he took us hunting; but he mentioned a spot where he wanted to eat lunch and was almost insistent although it seemed to be out of our way. He was a new acquaintance and I humored his whim.

It was a rather steep grade that the old Blazer clawed at briefly and then we were at the base of a butte, a flat-topped promontory thrust up at the edge of an immense sage flat that seemed to extend forever through thickening haze toward North Dakota. Around the stony base were Indian designs, many of them the reproductions of animal tracks, and there was the childish hacking of a few modern vandals.

Then we climbed to the top, a winding way of only a few yards and of no great difficulty although there were no steps.

And on the top, carefully designed to cover attack from any direction, were rifle pits—appearing haphazard at first, but laid out with geometric precision so that no attacker could approach the natural fortress unseen.

"No, I don't think Indians ever dug rifle pits in this country," Eustace said.

So who, I wanted to know, gouged out the deadly little trenches? It had been long, hard work. I waited for the answer. Ranchers fighting cattle thieves? Cavalry standing off Indians? Outlaws making a last stand against an awaited posse? Range war?

"I don't know who dug them and I can't seem to find out," Eustace said.

And I don't really want to know who did it. I have seen documented and landmarked battlefields.

Eustace looked off toward the Dakotas and endless sage.

"Certainly is good sage-hen country," he observed.

Gough Thomas, whose real name is G.T. Garwood of England, and who has written a lot of good stuff about shotguns, tells how Percy Stanbury, using a pumpgun, had five dead pigeons in the air simultaneously in the Teign Valley. Of course I had to buy Percy's book on shotgunnery and it's good, but the part that bothers me is that Stanbury was using a pumpgun in the first place and I have long thought that the British figured pumpguns and poisoned corn are in the same category.

Chapter Fifteen

You, Too, Can Be a Master Shotgunner

I missed the same quail four times on a single rise. I did this with a 20-gauge over-under Browning shotgun, which is unusual although I am sure many quail have been missed four times with autoloaders or pumpguns. By telling you how I missed the quail I hope to explain why I have long been interested in shooting schools and instruction and have become an authority on them.

I had known where the covey of quail lived for some time. They were what I call "swamp quail." Now swamp quail are not really a different species, but are simply bobwhites who have learned they are safer in swamps. There is a rumor that they always walk or wade and cannot fly but this is a silly idea since a swamp quail can fly like hell, being able to circle a cypress trunk in a tight bank at roughly 125 miles an hour. This is the reason why many swamp trees are mutilated by shot charges.

Quail living in really tight cover usually don't find much to eat back there and they generally come out to the edge to feed, probably in both morning and evening. If there is plenty of the proper seeds and greenery at the edge of the thick stuff a quail can comfortably fill his crop in a few minutes and scuttle back into the shadows. The covey I knew about was one of quite a number that hung out not far from town. I could not show you the place today because there is a shopping center there. I have tried to figure the exact spot where I missed the quail four times and as nearly as I can make out it is now the kitchenware section of a department store.

I used to take my old Brittany out late in the evening when the quail were outside the rough stuff and packing in the weed seeds. Old Kelly had it pretty well wired, figuring they would be within 50 feet of the edge, and he didn't waste much time farther out. Where he located the birds that evening they were at the border of a broom sedge field with no trees. Kelly specialized in suspense. When Kelly made game he did it with a breathless, conspiratorial attitude likely to reduce a nervous gunner to quivering protoplasm. After you followed him for a few vibrant yards he'd turn his head slowly toward you and check you over. The implication was:

"Man, they're here and you'd better be ready!"

He did that along the edge of the broom sedge, and since I was no rookie at this business I had things figured out. If the birds hadn't already heard us coming and scooted back into the woods they'd be sure to fly in there when they flushed. The first thought is to get between them and the heavy cover to cut them off—but that isn't so smart because they're probably pretty close to the edge and probably will fly right at you, freezing you with their beady little eyes and roaring like artillery shells. By this time I am sure you have perceived that bobwhite quail have my number—more so than ruffed grouse, Canada geese or intercontinental ballistic missles.

Anyway, I walked straight to where I figured the birds would be waiting, and they were, going up pretty well together, and although it appeared there were a couple hundred of them I think a dozen is a more accurate estimate. Most of them bored into the forest while I was sorting out the controls, finding the safety and trigger and getting a hazy view of the rib. But one bird was really stupid and so shook he didn't know which way to go. He headed right out across the broom sedge field about nine feet high.

My sub-conscious (the instructors explain that's what you shoot with) took charge at this point, noted that the open shot would be easiest and diverted my attention from the main covey and to the single boring off out of what is now the Kitchenware Department and over the Children's Wear Section. I was more than ready and missed him at approximately eleven feet, saw I had been in too much of a hurry and then missed him very carefully when he was almost out of range.

My reflexes broke the gun, the ejectors worked and I was subconsciously stuffing in two fresh shells when I saw the quail had noted his original error. Somewhere over Sporting

Goods he realized he was alone and that he was passing no protective trees so he made a 180-degree turn and headed straight toward me and the thick stuff. Disconcerted at this turn of events, I fired too soon while he was still pretty well out, then was very careful with my fourth shot, missing at about eleven feet again. At eleven feet and closing a flat-out bobwhite rooster can look menacing.

While all of these misses are excusable, I thought they should be mentioned as a background for my studious approach to shotgunnery, my attendance at shotgun schools and my attention to the experiences of a wide variety of shotgun masters. Not only am I obsessed by literature on how to shoot but I even love to watch the hotshots at work on skeet or trap fields. This sure beats a weakness for professional football or boxing as the seats are free and easily found. Shotgunnery isn't a spectacular sport but I don't think golf is either. All those people are confused.

When a trap or skeet shooter runs more than a thousand targets without missing I am impressed since I can't tap the end of my nose with my finger that many times without missing. And some of the game shooting achievements are almost as spectacular.

In a quail shooting tournament, Rudy Etchen killed five birds on a covey rise with his Remington pumpgun—and although I understand a good shucker can work one faster than an autoloader, I am disturbed about the pointing part. I have a pretty good Remington pumpgun with a figured walnut stock and every time I hear about things like what Etchen did I get it out and look at it. I know Etchen, and I have studied him carefully too, but except for being pretty big he looks like other people.

Gough Thomas, whose real name is G.T. Garwood of England, and who has written a lot of good stuff about shotguns, tells how Percy Stanbury, using a pumpgun, had five dead pigeons in the air simultaneously in the Teign Valley. Of course I had to buy Percy's book on shotgunnery and it's good, but the part that bothers me is that Stanbury was using a pumpgun in the first place and I have long thought that the British figured pumpguns and poisoned corn are in the same category.

The British, when shooting driven game, do not approve of repeaters ordinarily but have "loaders" standing behind them to hand up charged double guns as needed. This keeps a lonesome Purdey or Holland from getting too hot to handle, and while a repeater is considered a hoggish contraption a good loader can keep your double supplied with loaded chambers until either the birds or your shoulder gives out. I do not have a loader.

The Second Marquess of Ripon (England) kept track of his shotgunnery and killed more than half a million birds, dying of a heart attack in 1923 after knocking off his 52nd grouse of that day. My personal feeling is that the Maker had decided that was enough shooting for one guy, even a marquess.

Fred Kimble, using a singleshot muzzleloader, shot 1,365 ducks in 19 days, which was a heck of a stunt back in that other century, but when modern gunners shake their heads and say that no one can get that much game practice these days without living in England and being a duke or something they're just copping out. For the price of a vacation in the Black Hills you can go to Central America or South America and shoot at doves until you or your gun breaks. I have watched pretty good shooters knock off more than 100 in a morning or evening shoot in Honduras and in Colombia, where I never went, they say you needn't ever quit unless it gets dark. Some of those shooters get well over a thousand birds on a single trip so the Marquess of Ripon may have been outdone by eager-beaver dove poppers who don't keep track or report their sources, possibly because they don't want to keel over after batting down one last bird.

Now Captain A. H. Bogardus, who admitted to being the world's greatest at the time, would bet you that he could kill 100 snipe with 100 shells. Maybe he'd shoot two at once after a miss. I never had enough shells to kill 100 snipe.

Now, since current high-jumpers and weightlifters seem to have little trouble in outdoing those of years ago, I have no doubt that some of the shooters of today could wipe out the old timers, especially if they used modern guns and shells. Some skeet and trap shooters have such long runs of hits that a single tournament-losing miss may rate a whole page in their publications. Although most of them are pretty vague about how they do it I have unashamedly followed their instruction. Sometimes it is pretty humiliating.

Bob Carter has been a very discouraging contact concerning shotguns. I have avoided shooting where he was close enough to hear me but Carter was once a member of a world championship skeet team. He did his career in the Air Force and was a pilot. I have found that fliers, whether they are gunners or airplane drivers, are likely to be disgustingly good at winged game since they have been coached in "deflection shooting" and may have spent a great deal of time near skeet and trap ranges with unlimited ammunition. They have also had the incentive that involves being shot dead if they didn't shoot pretty good and pretty fast. I got the dope from Carter while bonefishing with him. As usual with such people, I asked questions regarding his reloading equipment, his experiences in competition and finally, his choice of guns for quail shooting.

Bob said he used a full-choke shotgun for quail, even in Florida brush, and I needed more information since the usual disagreement is whether a quail gun should be bored cylinder, skeet or improved cylinder. He explained that he shoots the first bird with just the edge of the pattern, then gradually moves in as the birds get farther away, finally centering the long ones with the pattern center. I knew something about this because I have always shot all quail with the edges of the pattern but had personally preferred improved cylinder. I am sure there were other things I could have learned from him but at the time I couldn't think of any more questions. I believe a bonefish came by. He can't catch bonefish any better than I can although he once trained a German shorthair to drive pheasants out of posted property for him.

I built a Crazy Quail pit many years ago—a clay pigeon trap located in a hole so that the targets can be thrown out at any angle, high or low. It was wonderful training but even the good shots made poor scores most of the time and one trap champion threw his custom over-under in the mud after missing eight straight. Finally, I was left alone with the setup, not because I was good but because nobody else would face the poor scores. Experts, I note, like to see them break.

So I mounted a practice trap where I could pull it myself with a long string and shoot from all angles. That was more than 20 years ago and I am now on my ninth practice machine. That first year I was getting ready to write a book on hunting upland birds and thought I had better learn to shoot. After shooting something like 14,000 rounds I could pull the string and break about two out of three. After 20 years of practice, I can now pull the spring and break about two out of three.

I went to skeet and trap ranges and listened to instruction, learning that shooters don't necessarily know how to teach although some do. Like a football coach who has never played football, it is hard for a bum shot to get the respect of his pupils. I got the full treatment from Fred Missildine, a trap and skeet champion, who runs his own school and really teaches instead of handing out rumors and telling how he did it. Fred helped me a lot and broke me from fooling around after I had a target lined up, which translated into faster shooting. Fred shoots American style, which means his left hand is fairly well back. The British teach you to shoot with your left hand (for a right-hander) pretty well extended and they swing the weight of the arm instead of the barrel—a fine distinction I have heard no one else mention—but if you'll practice it you'll see what I mean.

The British have the reputation of being the world's greatest game shots, largely because they shoot a lot of birds if they can afford it and shooting is pretty social over there. They say the forend of a double is just to hold the gun together and they often use a leather-covered handguard on the barrels so they can reach way out there toward the muzzle with a left hand without burning it. I have this English shotgun that I dearly love because it is short and quick, which partly makes up for my molasses swing, so I bought one of those leather handguards to show the boys I was the type who knows about tweed jackets and smells wine corks.

But every time I shot, the damned thing slipped on out toward the muzzle as the gun kicked and I gave it away because I was afraid my left hand might be across the muzzle for the second shot. I gave it to Ted Watson and I do not think he knew what it was. I told him it was a retainer for a two-handled posthole digger and I don't know what he did with it. He hits pretty good with a covey of British shotguns but he shoots them in a provincial style.

Well, the British way is probably best for some kinds of shooting and the American way probably wins at others. I don't want into that fuss but I know a nice lady who shoots a 20-gauge Winchester 21 and she has a custom forend that runs way out there where the leather handguard would go. She kills a lot of quail with it but it is too sensible for a real gun nut, who would much rather have the leather thing or a blistered hand.

Bruce Bowlen, who wrote the *Orvis Wing-Shooting Handbook*, sort of crosses the English dope with American systems. A veteran U.S. uplander who I thought would sneer at anybody's instruction, even if it appeared carved in stone during lightning flashes, memorized the Bowlen text and swears it has boosted his kill percentage, which was already sickening. It sort of louses up a hundred years of British scorn for the provincial American "riflemen with shotguns" but the two systems are getting pretty much alike, taking some fun out of the whole thing.

Anyway, the British are long on gun fit, stressing subconscious pointing and no attention to things like ribs and sights. There are, of course, marksmen who swear they never see the gun at all in wingshooting but, of course, they do see the barrel or barrels subconsciously or they couldn't hit with a strange gun.

The greatest tool for gun fit is the "try gun," which has an infinitely adjustable stock so that you can turn screw adjustments until it feels right. Unfortunately, an occasional stock fitter will sell somebody thousands of dollars worth of custom gun the customer must use for home defense while he goes back to hunting with the one that has rust on the receiver. I once knew all about gun fit and had all of mine (I have quite a number of shotguns, not because I collect them but because I kept thinking a new one would solve my problems) worked to the same dimensions. I had all sorts of tracings drawn on wrapping paper and had the drop at comb and heel, point of balance and stock length all figured out. Still, some of these guns wouldn't shoot worth a damn for me. I bought a custom Italian gun, which was made to my measure but wouldn't kill birds very well.

It was after the Italian gun and its pretty engraving had been sold for a miserable price to a friend who didn't really want it, that I discovered "pitch." Before then I'd known that pitch was the angle at which the barrels leave the stock. Lean the gun against the wall with the butt flat on the floor and the pitch is measured in the distance of the barrel from the wall. Since a little change in the recoil pad shape or a little mud on it can give an impression of great alteration in pitch, I figured it wasn't too important.

Then I got a gun that didn't match any of my custom whittled marvels in drop at comb or heel. Before I had it altered to the magic formula I went out and discovered I shot better with it than I did with most of the others. No changes. Then I checked the pitch and found there wasn't any. None. Then, while tossing fitfully, I realized that pitch can change almost anything and that bending a stock is likely to be just as good as carving it. I no longer tell my friends what kind of stock they need. I don't know what kind of stock *I* need.

And I concluded the way to get a gun that fits is to put it up with your eyes closed and then open them. If it's pointed in the general direction you are looking it ain't bad and drawing outlines on wrapping paper is a lot of work. Stock and forend *bulk* is seldom considered but is likely to make a big difference in how you shoot. This means that you may shoot a lot better with a light but bulky twelve gauge than with a toylike twenty-eight that you lose somewhere in the folds of your vest when you're in a hurry.

I morosely consider that I, myself, think I could help most shooters with their problems, convinced that although I can't do it myself I *know* how it *should* be done. Since almost everyone owning a shotgun feels he is a competent instructor, it is essential that those seeking shooting secrets be good judges of alleged experts.

I once went to a pretty big skeet shoot, planning to write something about it, and the management gave me the red carpet.

"I'll get someone to help you with anything you need," the man said, whereupon he produced a beautiful young lady carrying a shoot program and a devastating smile. She accompanied me to a good place on the bleachers (they're never crowded) and wanted to know if I'd like a cup of coffee.

In most circumstances I'd have been entranced by such companionship but in this case I was just a little miffed, feeling the host should have handed me over to some well-known competitor for a few minutes so that I could collect a quote or two of shooting wisdom. Instead, he'd obviously felt a girl-shaped girl would keep the old fud happier. Anyway, I muttered along with a monologue concerning my learned opinions on skeet shooting and the lady listened with wide-eyed attention.

"Of course," I expanded as I warmed to the subject, "the 28-gauge scores can't be expected to match anything done by the 20-gauge."

"Well, gee," she said, "I don't know. I broke a hundred with the twenty-eight when I took it at Phoenix last week."

There is a special humility that comes when I receive unsolicited instruction from someone I *know* is short on credentials but sees I am in need of help. There was the time in Honduras when I started slow at a dove shoot. My pickup boy (I should call him a *secretario* to show I'm a real international sport) had rushed me to a good spot before dawn and the birds were moving well. Other shooters banged away happily and doves were falling all over the place while pickup boys darted about noisily.

I believe I missed the first six birds. Anyway, my *secretario* was standing in a cloud of gloom at my side, looking forward to three days of embarrassing misses by his sport and wishing he were somewhere else. Finally, he yelled something in Spanish and held out his hands for my gun, which I surrendered. He then swung it to his shoulder and raked the sky briskly, shouting "Bang!" at intervals. Then he handed it back to me with words which obviously meant, "See what I mean?"

Now just what gunning breakthrough he was demonstrating I do not know but it happened that I got the next dove that passed and did pretty well for the rest of the morning—for me, which means maybe one bird for three shots. Every time I stole a look at the *secretario* he was beaming with fatuous self-satisfaction, sure he had taught the fundamentals to a rank beginner. Every *paloma* he picked up was a personal triumph for his instructional system and each hit came with enthusiastic cheers and congratulations.

I know all about shotgun teachers.

Your feet learn to grope for the little creeks that may be hidden during this high water, and you learn to stay away from the shoulder-high brush tangles or rotting stumps where water moccasins take the sun streaks on cool days. On a quiet morning in the swamp a pileated woodpecker sounds like a lonely roofer with an imminent deadline, and the little red-bellied sapsuckers make delicate scratching sounds as they go circling up the cypress trunks with furtive glances at a slow-moving hunter slipping along beneath them. There are owls in there and occasional gray squirrels.

Chapter Sixteen

Swamp Woodies

It took all week to find where the wood ducks fed every evening, and the hunt was drawing to a close when I began my part. I met Buddy Nordmann as he closed his store, and we rode his Land Rover out of town and across the river bridge to take a lane that slipped through the scattered pines and thick palmettos and erased the sight and sound of highway traffic.

The Rover's slow-turning four cylinders sounded louder back there in the late afternoon quiet, British and permanent. The old Rover still runs these years later, despite the inroads of seashore rust on some of the underparts and the scaling, grey-greenish paint. Parts are a little hard to find since England declined to compete with America's clawing four-wheel-drive behemoths, the gleaming ones with roll bars and lights sitting up there on a level with tree limbs. *Bubba trucks* we call the macho rigs with the gesturing CB aerials and the enormous tires.

That evening we stopped in a clearing and watched the sky over Florida's big river, the St. Johns, a waterway full of yachts and skiffs and tugs and barges, but only a dark line of oak and cypress from where we stood by the little truck. It was almost sundown when we saw the first birds, two of them, going with the purposeful speed of traveling ducks, well above the dark river line.

To me they could have been any breed of waterfowl, but I used the binoculars and steadied the wavering images into wood duck silhouettes against the sky, head just a little high and the tail looking long and pointed. They passed, became specks and disappeared.

"We've just about got them now," Nordmann said, as much to his wildlife memory bank as to me. All week he had been watching the ducks in the ancient process used by bee hunters looking for a swarm, watching a little further along the route each evening.

He stood and pieced together the wood duck route, from the river swamp where they had spent the day, up through the cypress canopy and out over the river where they settled on their straight course, over the new housing development and the ferneries and orange groves, over some small lakes where the water gleamed in streaks between shoals of lily pads, and then down to some feeding spot he hadn't located positively but was almost sure of.

He thought his way across the route he was almost sure of, calling on knowledge of the area that he began collecting when he was a boy with an old hammer shotgun and a mail-order casting reel.

"That's where it'd almost have to be," he mumbled, and watched two more wood ducks, and then a little bunch and more little groups, all of them on the same route and at nearly the same height. Then a few, an important few, came past from a slightly different angle, probably from a different swamp. That triangulated it, and Buddy got back into the Land Rover.

"I'll check 'em in tomorrow night and the next day we'll shoot 'em," he said.

Three of us went out on shooting day and for the first time during the week-long hunt Buddy had his shotgun. The other gunner was Milt Culp, a young swamp lover in perpetually wet tennis shoes, who had helped with the watching. Buddy drove down a country road to where the oaks were especially tall, and we got out in our camouflaged jackets.

"Just a little piece back in here."

There were leaves and forest debris on the ground, and there were acorns, thousands of acorns. Milt walked on a little farther and, as the guest, I stopped with Buddy. Buddy's Lab sat beside us, yellow-eyed and expectant. Light was getting a little dull where we were but sun still struck the treetops.

Buddy stood with his gun open and talked about dove shooting and black bass. I half listened and looked up at the patch of sky above us, fiddled with the twenty-gauge shells in the pocket of my jacket and felt a little foolish—like a kid with a corn sack waiting for a snipe. But this was daylight and the people who had set up the hunt were waiting with me—or at least I assumed Milt Culp hadn't sneaked on out of the forest and back to town.

"We should have about two minutes to shoot before sundown," Buddy said. "That's enough. After that it'd be illegal."

I looked at my watch, as if it meant anything to me. It was three minutes until legal sundown, my watch said, and Buddy clicked shut his gun and stepped over near a tree trunk.

"You're in a good place," he said. Jet, the Lab, seemed to appraise my position before joining Buddy by the oak.

I fumbled the yellow shells into the little five-and-a-quarter-pound Sauer double, certainly nobody's idea of a duck gun, but Buddy had said they'd be right in my lap and darting.

"No big deal, but kind of quick," he said, or something like that.

His-s-s-s-s-s! came the ducks through the little opening over us, their wings set momentarily and their tails spread like fans to break their speed. Their wings sputtered then as they saw us and they changed course with squeals, only two or three birds I think, but others were just behind them. I punched the little gun toward a gaudy drake, too close to me, lost him behind a leafy branch, didn't shoot, found another and missed as he stopped and towered. I'm a little vague about the rest.

"Fetch!" ordered Buddy with his special inflection and Jet brought four wood ducks to us, our legal limit, while birds continued to squeal, flutter and hiss through oaks and I tried to figure how many shells I had used. The sun was down and Milt walked up with his birds, the hunt over as if some director had called, "Cut!"

It is different in the dull-lighted river swamp where the birds are scattered during midday and black water is only a few inches deep, the cypress forest made up partly of knees standing like crouching creatures from some underwater world. There are fallen trees and limbs and truly ancient stumps from the long ago when long saws and cranky machinery took cypress from the swamp for the first time.

Your feet learn to grope for the little creeks that may be hidden during this high water, and you learn to stay away from the shoulder-high brush tangles or rotting stumps where water moccasins take the sun streaks on cool days. On a quiet morning in the swamp a pileated woodpecker sounds like a lonely roofer with an imminent deadline, and the little red-bellied sapsuckers make delicate scratching sounds as they go circling up the cypress trunks with furtive glances at a slow-moving hunter slipping along beneath them. There are owls in there and occasional gray squirrels.

There was one morning when I stopped to listen to a sound that did not fit, a steady splash of approaching feet in four inches of water, and I instinctively drew back against a tree trunk, just a little nervous about an unknown traveler in a half-lighted forest. It was the largest southern whitetail buck I have ever seen. He stared at me from 40 yards, turned and stalked away. After he left I listened to the distant song of the hounds that had moved him.

But it is the wood ducks you look for, and you travel as quietly as possible. When Buddy Nordmann used to take old Jet through the swamp he would whisper for her to heel, but when Jet finally became too nervous and tried to walk past him he would thunk her skull gently with the barrel of his Model 12 Winchester. It didn't seem to disturb the ducks.

You listen for the conversational whistling and cheeping of ducks, and if you hear it up ahead, you are especially quiet. Sometimes the ducks are scattered and you can't tell just where, because a cypress swamp has its own acoustics. There is a lingering fear that you'll scare up birds you can't even see, however close, and when you approach a flooded patch of brush with wood duck sounds coming from it you wish you had the other gun—either the open bird gun or the duck gun, depending upon which you don't have with you. I have never once felt I had the right one except the time I dropped my over-under in a foot of swamp water and was afraid to fire it afterward. Incidentally, that was on a weekend with no gun repair available, the water was a bit brackish, and I became an instant gunsmith (momentarily terrorized) at the sight of my clumsily dismantled pet upon the kitchen table.

Generally the water's surface is calm, even if there is a

breeze in the cypress crowns, and you strain for sight of the gentle wavelets far ahead, betraying unseen ducks behind tree trunks, brush or blowdowns. When the light is right the little wakes show for a hundred yards or more. Then you slip from tree to tree, feeling huge and awkward.

When they go up they are more disconcerting than swift; and because their takeoff is scattered in the swamp, a sizable flock can keep a flustered gunner rejecting target after target as nearer birds appear. But it is the wood duck's broad tail that ruins the expert's swing. He flies at a tree trunk, turns down his combination of flaps and rudder, stands almost erect in midair and makes a right-angled turn. Then comes his flat-out acceleration through the branches, accompanied by startled screams. Only a wood duck knows what his new direction will be.

But a hunter can be clever. Peering past an enormous tree trunk, I sighted a drake and hen swimming directly toward me a full hundred yards away, paddling along rapidly. This had never happened before and I smirked as I slipped back of the tree, knowing I must wait until time to shoot before stepping out before the horrified drake. They swam faster than I expected, and as I prepared to emerge I realized with discomfiture that their wavelets showed directly opposite me on the other side of my tree.

I stepped out, feeling for my shotgun and composure. It seemed like a whole flock of wood ducks spattering into the air ten feet from my boots, and I shoved the muzzle at one of them. It was a hen. Why shoot a hen when a fat drake was hanging virtually motionless before me? I swung on the drake, fired and ripped down a small limb as he ducked behind a tree. I leaped to one side and sighted him again, flying straight at a curtain of foliage. My second shot was well ahead because he stopped in midair to survey his escape route. At least the leaves I severed made his exit easier.

Whatever the woodie is noted for, it is not speed—at least in the books that record waterfowl ballistics. I do not know how fast he flies uphill but when he power dives he becomes a projectile. Even a buzzard can approach the sound barrier if he is headed down. I learned about wood duck speed just after dawn.

I knew they came into a swamp early after feeding some-place known only to people like Buddy Nordmann. I anchored the skiff in a narrow backwater and I had it right. I hoped that some birds would come in almost over me, and they did. They came with a whistling roar of wings, diving from high altitude to enter the swamp's cypress. I sat and missed, groping in the sky ahead of them for the lead needed to intercept a cannonball. Only the whistling dive of a reckless merganser or ringneck seemed to parallel their speed. Their performance was not typical, but then neither was mine. I bagged one. .

Off the St. Johns there is a side channel bordered on one side by oaks. Culp and I pulled our skiff against the bank, secure in the knowledge the birds would hover over us before landing. Again the flight pattern had been scouted by some-one else, and I was indebted to Milt. At first I could pay him back by taking him snook fishing. Then, of course, he learned the way to snook fishing himself.

We had no true blind, but the boat was tight against a two-foot bank. And some Spanish moss, aided by a few small rafts of water hyacinths Milt's young chessie tried to walk across, broke the silhouette. When you wait quietly you are surprised by the whispers of "silent" hyacinth rafts rubbing together as they move in a slow current along with their little community of tiny living things, possibly with little bluegills or warmouths plucking at them with little sucking sounds from underneath.

A flock of white ibis swept low along the dark channel avenue, avoiding the disturbing air currents above the tree-tops. Their wings whispered lightly, and they swerved up-ward and away as they saw two men and a bug-eyed Chesa-peake watching them. Along with several white birds were several blotchy ones—youngsters still carrying some of the dark brown feathers of youth.

Then, while Milt was trying to reason with the pup, who was remarkably set in his ways for so young a dog, a single drake wood duck buzzed the narrow channel lengthwise, power on and retaining speed from his high altitude dive. I swung so fast and hard I came around as if I had used a bat instead of a shotgun and, wonder of wonders, the drake hit the water so hard he skipped.

Then some jabbering woodies came in the way they were supposed to and we got a couple more. The next year that setup was no good at all, for they fed elsewhere.

I like to see wood ducks in Florida's little woodland lakes that are generally trimmed in rushes, lily pads and palmetto. You can locate those forest ponds from a distance by the circular pattern of the tree crowns, and the woodies generally surprise you when you're deer or quail hunting, squealing as they leave for some other lake. Unfortunately, there are no cases in which backwoods ponds are so brushy that wood duck hunting gets easy, and meat seekers wade into the midst of roosting areas, ignoring the sundown cease-fire law.

The smaller a roost lake and the higher the timber about it, the more dramatic the wood duck arrival as darkness closes. Wood ducks have a sporting way of coming in with a controlled fall, rudder tails spread and looking like bundles of carelessly assembled feathers in silhouette.

Final arrivals at a roosting pond can be late enough that most of the sunset color has faded, too late even for the illegal shooters. I once visited such a pond to watch the roosting flight, looking expectantly into a sky with silhouetted swinging moss and cypress tops.

I waded in as far as my boots would allow, contemplated wading wet, but decided it was too chilly. The early-comers were sedate in their arrivals, swinging in like ordinary ducks and assembling in little pods with excited discussions. They did not notice me among the rushes in my camouflaged jacket. It was later that the aerobatics started.

When the really tardy birds came they fell in from the starry sky as hurtling blobs, striking hard sometimes. One actually splashed water in my face, recognized me as an unfamiliar obstacle and took off again with high-pitched warnings, unheeded by the other birds, who made sounds I had never heard from ducks. They fussed, expressed endearment, fought and grumbled.

It was black dark when I got out of there and, as is common in our part of the country, another nature lover found the pond with an open-bored twelve-gauge automatic a few days later and killed all he could carry. They haven't roosted there since.

Wood ducks make swamps better.

"Pictures of a dog retrieving trout are touchy business," said a fishing editor. "With the catch-and-release thing going strong a fish retriever would be suspected of damaging the fish and the trout public will yell."

Chapter Seventeen

Fishing Dogs

J ohn Rucker is a brilliant writer who has a friend named Barney. Barney is a springer spaniel who has traveled the continent with John and has helped him hunt from Alaska south. Rucker has written beautiful prose about his travels and his sensitive photographs often feature Barney—photographs made in Alaska where Barney monitored John's salmon nets and retrieved big rainbows that John caught on flies, and photographs made much farther south where Barney observed angling operations with intensity, even when the caster was a total stranger.

"Pictures of a dog retrieving trout are touchy business," said a fishing editor. "With the catch-and-release thing going strong a fish retriever would be suspected of damaging the fish and the trout public will yell."

Maybe, but Barney didn't dent the trout and other fish retrievers have done it gently too. I never found a mark on the trout that old Tex retrieved, even when the actual capture was a welter of flying water. Don't know how he did it.

Tex, the deep-chested old Brittany who was a disaster at bird retrieving, (tending to hide them from me) classified fish retrieving differently. He observed each cast with critical appraisal and stared accusingly at me when I caught nothing. Tex was intolerant. We used to fish a mountain lake filled with rainbows, wading in just far enough to cover drop-offs with flies, and when a fish took, Tex would prick his ears. From then on he got a little jumpy and was inclined to crash into the water while the fish was still green. But if you could keep him under control until the proper time he'd bring out the fish with almost as much dignity as Barney.

We'd never let Tex go along for stream fishing but sometimes we'd have him with us in a boat. His interest in a plug retrieve was so intent that he'd lean farther and farther over the gunwale. At intervals he'd simply fall in, even if there was no fish, and retrieving him was a wet chore, pretty unpleasant when the water was cold. Then, of course, he'd shake. On one day when he'd already been fished out two or three times I announced that next time we'd leave him in there a while to teach him a little more caution. The boat's sides were fairly high.

A little later, while Tex was engrossed in the maneuvers of a Rapala over a bassy eelgrass patch, there was the distinctive plop that meant Tex had leaned too far and I saw him paddling easily and looking demandingly upward for rescue.

"Pay no attention to him," I ordered. "We'll let him swim until he's a little tired and teach him a lesson."

Feeling a little guilty I made a cast at the eelgrass and watched the plug for a moment. From the corner of my eye I saw Tex investigating the boat's waterline with disgust and then heading toward the stern. I turned away and cast again. Halfway through that retrieve I felt the familiar spatter of cold water on my back and there was Tex shaking himself, having climbed on the transom (I guess) and squirmed past the outboard motor where I didn't think there could have been room.

Since climbing against an outboard motor is a little like crawling over a bag of bayonets, I checked Tex for abrasions and found none but my wife and I agreed that however he had managed the boarding operation it was dangerous. Anyway, we said, he'd learned a lesson and we shouldn't have to fish him out any more. Tex appeared coldly aloof but moved to the gunwale to watch the plugs work. He edged a little farther out. A coot flew from a nearby clump of emergent arrowhead, a surprise to Tex. Plop! I reached out and grabbed his collar. I know when I'm whipped.

Licking a freshly-caught fish is a ritual insisted upon by several dogs we've taken along in a boat. If the fish is big the lick might be quick and furtive but is generally accomplished, even if the licker has his feet tuned for escape and his eyes bulging. Kelly, who always licked fish, was especially excited if one jumped and splashed. Since tarpon do all of this with a flair, his first experience with a good-sized tarpon was an emotional experience.

The fish was hooked on a streamer fly and continued to jump at close quarters, provoking warning whines and choppy barks from Kelly. To release it I had to drag it aboard with a lip gaff and while I did that I noted that Kelly had disappeared. As the fish came noisily aboard he had retired to the stern were he took refuge behind a canvas boat seat—reminding me of the landing craft sailor who had hidden under a canvas cot during a bombing raid. The sailor said he knew the canvas was no protection but didn't want to be reminded of it.

Anyway, Kelly peered apprehensively with one big eye around the side of the seat. The hero of various canine brawls and fearless confrontations with meter readers and letter carriers had abandoned me in the face of danger. I had thought better of Kelly's heroism but I had not counted on the difference between sensible caution and response to life-and-death situations.

As I twisted at the hook with a pair of fisherman's pliers the fish gave a mighty flop, its tail coming up near my face. This, Kelly felt, was a clearcut attack upon the boat's captain. A brindle missile flashed past me with furious snarls and Kelly was atop the tarpon, gnashing wildly at its scaled armor. Where is a tarpon's throat?

The release of a fish was puzzling to Kelly. I have no doubt that he approved of the sportsmanship involved but he never figured where a fish goes when turned loose. Anyway, if you released a fish four feet ahead of the stern on the port side, Kelly would check that section of the gunwale at intervals all day, no matter how far we traveled. He would peer down into the water and even reach toward it with a paw now and then. In a very small boat where he could reach the water he'd swish his paw around in it a little. I do not consider this one of Kelly's more brilliant moves and recount it with some embarrassment but console myself that this is another example of my understanding something he didn't. There have been other times when he made me feel inferior.

In wading trout streams I have found myself remarkably able to get along without canine assistance. When I've allowed a bird dog to accompany me on such trips I have usually regretted it.

I took old Kelly the Brittany on a few wading expeditions, feeling a little streamside exploration would bolster his morale during the long closed season for bird specialists. There was one memorable trip involving a considerable hike to a tiny creek, little more than a chain of pools, none more than two feet deep, coming down out of the mountains and bordered by cover that often held a ruffed grouse or two. Like other pools of their depth, some of these must be approached with care and I sometimes got on my knees to keep a low silhouette for spooky trout vulnerable to land-based predators. As soon as Kelly saw me wade into one of the longer pools he grasped the drill and splashed ahead of me at high speed for something like a quarter mile.

But the late Dan Bailey, one of the great trout anglers, was regularly accompanied by a Labrador. The Baileys owned several generations of them and they waded or swam around Dan through the years. They were pretty well trained but when one's exuberance got out of hand Dan thought it was very amusing to see a pool ruined. Dan Bailey was mild-tempered.

If we all judged hunting dogs by the same standards, most of them would be out of a job and some breeds would be sent to the pound en masse.

Chapter Eighteen

A New Breed

I am the guy who gave up on a pointer I couldn't handle and then read where he had won a national field trial after I had given him away. That's right. No charge.

Without discounting my own stupidity about canines I still don't want Magnificent Murphy back because even if he won every field trial honor in the book I still couldn't use him. Murphy and I had different philosophies. I bought him to run big in open country—but not as big as he did. For all I know he may have hunted part of the time where the season wasn't even open and in those days he'd get lost and howl until I trudged to the scene of his embarrassment, whereupon he'd take off again before I could catch him. I considered shooting him but I couldn't get within range when I was in the mood.

Not only did Murph fail in getting me shots at birds, he ran out all the game before more considerate and less athletic dogs could get there. When he pointed it was too far away to tell what he had and by the time I could get near he would have become disgusted, busted his birds and gone on to conquer other worlds. When a man with an electric collar and a good quarter horse got on his trail he began to win field trials. I wish him the best of luck, and hope I never see him again.

If we all judged hunting dogs by the same standards, most of them would be out of a job and some breeds would be sent to the pound *en masse*.

Top dogs are inclined to be specialists. I knew a champion skeet shot who had trained a poaching dog that ran into posted cornfields and chased the pheasants out to where he could shoot them. The man was thus a contributor to canine delinquency, making a criminal of a well-bred pointer, and I have often wondered if such degraded instincts could be made hereditary. Imagine a shoplifting poodle or a Great Dane that mugged people in alleys.

Specialized dogs are the real wonders, but I am as much impressed by those that adapt to a variety of situations. My Brittany, Kelly, although not very staunch as a pointer and infuriating as a non-retriever, worked all of the North American varieties of upland game and while other dogs may have done it, I haven't heard of them. He managed it so you got the shots, even while some of his tactics would make perfectionists weep.

Another Brittany named Michael McGillicuddy is as stylish as high button shoes but has figured out a lot of things above and beyond the call of duty. I once planned to steal him but felt it would be like kidnaping Albert Einstein and would probably give me an insurmountable inferiority complex.

In addition to his other accomplishments McGillicuddy has figured out some mind-boggling pheasant tactics. For the benefit of you disadvantaged peasants who have never hunted ringnecks, they tend to run rather than fly and have sent many a polished pointing dog to a psychiatrist. McGillicuddy knows about this and when he nails a pheasant in thick brush he figures that as the gunner comes up the bird will probably run rather than take off.

So as you approach from McGillicuddy's stub-tailed rear he will look over his shoulder to make sure you are ready and then just as you come abreast of him he jumps straight up into the air and says, "*Grr-r-r-row!*" The pheasant squawks and goes and if you don't hit him it's your fault and McGillicuddy goes off to find another one. He reasons that going straight up is not breaking a point, a philosophy that might cause a bit of confusion among field trial judges.

McGillicuddy, incidentally, was entered once in a field trial and disgraced his owner. At the "breakaway" he amiably admired the judges' horses and refused to engage in any childish racing about. He did find and point all of the bobwhites that had been planted in the "bird field" but the damage was already done. Field trial dogs are not supposed to fraternize with the gallery.

Now I have hunted with three ruffed grouse dogs that bark when a grouse flies into a tree. This isn't unusual, I understand, and it's a good trick where I've hunted ruffs in the West. When the dog points a grouse the bird is likely to become bored with such classic tomfoolery and flutter up into the nearest tree, sometimes to sit on a lower branch and inspect the intruder. Since you might not be able to see any of this activity because of thick brush, a couple of yips from your helper are welcome.

Among the efficient but nonconformist southern dogs are the palmetto prodders, generally English pointers. I have seen some of them do their stuff—although I never met George, who I have heard was the acknowledged master of the process.

George would point just as well as any Fancy Dan aristocrat when the covey was in a reasonable spot. Then when the bunch split up and scattered into thick palmettos, George would put on his work clothes, so to speak, and sniff them out one by one and boost them up with his nose.

Since he could point until the season closed without being found in those palmettos, George adopted a logical procedure and no trap club ever enjoyed better presented targets then those George produced one at a time. Such tactics have been used, of course, by springer spaniels and even Labradors, but they don't point the covey to begin with.

Diversity of hunting methods and areas has led to some really wild escapades by breeders, some of whom have produced wondrous things and some of whom have fouled up the whole business.

The English setter, of course, is one of the finest bird dogs, generally having a bit more affection than the pointer and wearing a longer coat for rough going. But after you hear the objectives of the various breeders you wonder at the things that are happening to the poor old setter.

Originally, I think, he was intended as a close-going workman you could follow without track shoes. Then, when some setter owners found that the pointers ran faster and farther, they began breeding to meet the competition. The result was that for some time many setters competed on even terms with pointers and took home some of the shinier hardware in the classic field trials. A few still do it although pointers seem to have the edge there and I find the phenomenon of hunters trying to turn the setters around and take them back to their former style.

In getting them slower and closer, some breeders have made them bigger—one hell of a lot bigger. I am continually startled when approaching the home of a friend of mine to be met by a setter which weighs 90 pounds when he's just had a good meal—and although I like to look *down* instead of *up* at dogs when I'm seated on a divan, I know that this canine mastodon comes from a line of dogs bred for close work and may have cost as much as all of the dogs I've owned put together.

Now the German Shorthair, for example, is traditionally a heavy, slow-going plodder if you don't approve of him and a big, cautious, tight worker if you like him. But some shorthair owners looked around, decided the English pointer had something they didn't and apparently let some speedy Englishmen under the kennel fence. The result has been some fine dogs that look like English pointers with shortened tails, go like the milltails of hell and often have the biddability commonly associated with the more deliberate shorthair. Not everybody was satisfied with that and I've talked to some people who'd like to slow them down a little and head back in the original direction.

On the other hand, the Brittany spaniel is a pretty good pointing dog and was booked as an "old man's dog" that wouldn't lose you if your feet were sore. He's supposed to be highly adaptable and my experience is that although he may not have the nose of the pointer, he's usable at almost anything and is easy to live with because he weighs around 35 pounds.

But even I wanted one that would go a little wider sometimes and ended up with one that's too big to make the Brittany book and has lumpy muscles all over him. Just as I was basking in the admiration of people who appreciated my biggie, I heard of a new strain of Brittanies built for big country and hard going. I found the man who was breeding them and he showed me a beautiful dog that made mine look like a clod but appeared decidedly setterish. He weighed about 45 pounds, same as mine.

"This is one of the smaller ones," the breeder said. "We

want a Brittany that can be seen above the weeds and that will go all day. Some of ours weigh 70 pounds.

He has some fine dogs but his ideal is beginning to sound remarkably like an English pointer with a short tail and hair like a setter.

There is no harm in any of this and the result is that you can find almost anything you want that looks like something else if you'll investigate far enough. It's a little like the guy who buys an improved cylinder shotgun because he wants it to scatter and then brags that it really throws full-choke patterns.

Time was, of course, when a Chevrolet was a Chevrolet without any other names appended, and then came the time when you could get a Chevrolet with more power than a Cadillac. And the car dealer will tell you that his compact car is really larger than the competition's compact—or that his big car is really smaller and handier than the competition's big one.

All of the dog business is confusing to anyone who isn't aiming at something definite for his specific job. He may be surprised to find a German Shorthair that goes over the horizon and an English pointer that makes him bowlegged by walking between his feet.

Maybe they should shake the breed names in a basket.

"Whoa!" I yelled. It was a word evidently unknown to Mike. He had never heard it while working garbage cans in the alleys of his youth. It is possible he confused it with "Charge!" or possibly he considered it a sort of universal rebel yell.

I do not like to dwell on what happened next and I am going to state it with composure and as briefly as possible.

Chapter Nineteen

Chukars Forever

The shotguns I have used for chukar hunting have scratched and dented stocks, some of the more impressive wounds reminding of particularly humiliating stumbles and falls in lonely places. Writers have long made comedy of chukar chasing and American chukars are short on tradition, which takes time to develop.

Almost a hundred years ago the first chukars came to America but it was half a century after that before they were hunted here, a long history of unsuccessful introductions. It was not until after World War II that they became game for the few American dogs and gunners who followed them through the land they finally adopted, land that seemed of little use for anything else.

The red-legged partridges came from arid mountains across most of the world, from Spain to China, and when they settled in Hawaii and the United States their territory had encircled the globe. Most of the American chukars came from Asia and it was hard for us to believe they would not prefer better living quarters than those they left. We tried them in nearly every state and they finally chose dry and crumbling mountains with cheatgrass, sage and scattered juniper. Since much of the country they use is called "wasteland," it may be that when pheasant and quail habitat is largely covered by concrete and asphalt the chukar will still look down on unending cities from some rocky spine and pronounce his name.

There are Asiatic places where chukars are domestic birds, carried about in wicker cages and hawked in the markets. There are even chukar fighting cocks. Visit a zoo where chukars live at leisure, and although they retain their gray and black military uniforms they become oversized and portly. Chukars adapt.

A close relative of our chukars, the red-legged partridge of Spain, (they look almost the same) is hunted in the grand way. A corps of beaters will drive the birds down from mountains much like those of Nevada or Oregon and the gunners will wait in butts or blinds with practiced loaders to keep their double-guns running.

I have often thought of that when I have paused on a talus slope with sweat stinging my eyes, with my dog becoming pigheaded and with the soft clacking sounds of chukar talk far up ahead where the rimrock is in broken sections. I have never been to Spain but they say the birds are generally herded downhill in mountain winds with a full head of steam and that the shooting can be wild. The way I do it may not be better. It is different.

Asiatic tribesmen are responsible for the horse and whip system, the whip being for the chukars and not the horses. As I understand it, the riders charge into a flock of running chukars (even a chukar can't outrun an Asiatic version of the quarter horse) and kill them with the whips as they flush or scatter on the ground. Now this report brings laughter for some who have neither whips nor horses but I can see how it would work if you know your way with a saddle and have a quick horse who doesn't give a damn.

Chukars are great watchers and perhaps this is why they preferred mountains to Kansas wheatfields. You can't see much from a wheatfield when you're less than a foot tall.

I began chukar hunting when my wife said she thought she had seen one looking down from a stone perch to check our truck as it jounced along a double track. The dog and I pursued it as a novelty. The lookout hopped off the rock and disappeared in some cheat grass. Somewhere near there the dog pointed and I killed my first chukar after a startled miss or two. Many years and five chukar states later I have admitted addiction. I have worn out some boots and christened several of those skinned-up shotguns and I have developed a sentimental taste for arid hills where weather is generally too hot or too cold and frequently windy.

Those chukar lookouts (or are they just sightseers?) are one of the colorful parts of the program, especially when they're on high rimrock, and my wife is continually sighting them from the truck before or after a hunt. Sometimes I wish she would look for something else for I have learned that a chukar in the hand is worth 40 or 50 on the rocks.

I was with Fred Terwilliger when he sighted his first sentry from a jeep trail, just short of the spot where we planned to hunt. Now we are not road hunters. This is different. Fred got out with one eye on the chukar and one eye on his equipment. He moved stealthily and slightly uphill toward the sentry rock. His twenty snapped shut on a pair of three-inch shells with seven-and-one-half shot and the chukar said, "Chuka-r-r-r." He said it conversationally and I doubt if those Spanish shooters with the tweed jackets have any opportunity for such eyeball confrontations.

Twenty feet from the bird, and facing it at eye level, Fred was aware of something moving near his feet, and thinking of rattlesnakes, he looked down to find another chukar there—this one appearing upset. Since Fred had no beaters with him and I was watching tensely from the truck he knew it was time for the birds to fly so he said some loud things about chukars, ran a little and stamped his feet. Then there was the rustle of many chukar feet, the sentry hopped daintily down from his perch, and the whole damned flock disappeared into the mountain. Forever, I guess, for we never saw them again. Our dogs could smell chukars all right but they couldn't find them.

By this time I was with Fred, ready for action after trying to load some shells rim-first. Then, in typical chukar style, a dozen birds sailed in unheralded from across the canyon and landed in rimrock 200 feet above us. This was simpler. So we climbed above the rimrock and our dogs moved down to it and pointed. The birds came out in singles and pairs and after missing one at approximately eight feet I settled down and got one while Fred did a little better. I mused that we might have done better with horses and long whips.

I expect strange things to happen in chukar country. It was in the Owyhee country of southwestern Idaho that Mac the Brittany embarrassed himself. "Owyhee" is not an Indian name. It is a misspelled version of Hawaii and if you pronounce it aloud it comes out about right. It is not your run-of-the-mill crossroads. A long time ago some Hawaiian immigrants disappeared forever in that country. I am sorry that the jeep trails are beginning to look well used but it isn't too far from Boise and other people places.

I was picking my way along a rock slide, stumbling now and then among chukar-sized rocks and occasionally hearing the soft ventriloquil calls of chukars above me. It happened that old Mac, Fred's dog, was close to me while my own dog and Fred were up above somewhere, working along the same slope. Fred's 20-gauge whacked above me and I set my feet for what I was pretty sure would happen and did.

The little bunch of chukars came hissing down the slope, gaining speed, their blurred wings still driving as they had not yet started their mountainside glide. I swung the gun barrel a ridiculously long way ahead and one of the birds folded and tumbled down the slope below the others—out of sight in scattered sage.

Mac hadn't seen it and I yelled, "Dead bird!" while I stumbled down that way hoping it wasn't a cripple for a crippled chukar is very bad news. Mac came on the double, head down in a noisy snuffle because high, dry desert air isn't helpful for scenting. Within a minute he pointed and I hurried toward him, fearing the bird might be able to fly, but it wasn't. I saw it plainly, dead in the slide rock, shaded by a sage bush. It was plain to me but Mac, like other dogs, is supposed to be color blind and rocks and bird looked the same to him. He broke his point and appeared to dive at the bird but he couldn't see it and he grabbed the thing that *did* show a profile in the right place—one of the rocks the bird had struck in falling and two inches from the bird itself.

Mac turned to retrieve the rock, realized what he had and spit it out, decided he'd blown the whole thing and went looking for birds somewhere else, leaving my chukar under the sage bush. I picked it up, stuffed it into my vest and mused that anything could happen in a place named Owyhee.

Chukar hunters are inclined to draw maps in the dust and make long-distance calls at odd hours. The directions can get a little complicated.

I had a call from Tom Curtis while he was streaking across some southwestern state with a pickup truck, a Model 12

Winchester with a rib and a pointer named Smokey. Already, he was a long way from his Texas home. The call was similar to the ones I'd had the year before. Same subject: what was new on chukars in Idaho? Tom starts for chukars and then calls me to learn what I've heard. Maybe he figures if a plague had wiped out most of the species and he called from home before leaving that I'd stop him—and he wants to go anyway.

The year before, he had called several times while on the way. He found the general chukar location while he and Smokey were in New Mexico and I believe he got the exact spot while they were in Colorado—or maybe Wyoming. I'd had to do some checking between his calls. For a guy who has pulled down on all those quail, pheasants, Huns and geese Tom's condition amounts to addiction.

Well, this time I didn't have the very latest but my old friend Howie did and I turned Tom over to him. Tom, with a long career of following directions to things like goose flocks or quail coveys, will get there if the forecast sounds good.

Howie did himself proud. He named an Idaho town and he told of the highway out of town and the side road you take at a certain distance and how you would go to the right at the fork and past the ranch house and through the gate and so on, the kind of directions hunters and fishermen listen to all of their lives and treasure, even when they're written on old shell boxes or BLM maps.

I got a report from Tom a week later. It hadn't been quite what he'd expected, he said, but he followed the directions to the letter past the ranch house and down the long hill. That was where he had a little trouble because he never was able to find the old windmill. But he found some pretty good looking country and put Smokey down. It wasn't long before Smokey found some Hungarian partridges and Tom had a pretty good shoot.

"But I guess the chukars had moved," Tom said. "We just couldn't find them there so we came back to Boise and started over."

I reported this to Howie and Howie said he wasn't particularly anxious to discuss the trip with Tom.

"The fact is," Howie said, "I made a little mistake in giving the directions. At first I couldn't figure how he missed the windmill but I finally figured that I sent him to the wrong town. He should have gone a hundred miles further before turning off on the dirt road."

Maybe "triangulation" is too important a name for it but one of the best ways to locate chukars is from above and the tactic develops so gradually that you begin to suppose all hunters should know it. After doing it you begin to scorn the road hunters who bounce birds at waterholes. I went in September when the early Idaho season was hot and dry and bird dogs gave bored and panting attention to jack rabbits.

My birds didn't call much, just an occasional ventriloquil query from somewhere up a jagged little canyon with a few willows in the bottom. You could hear them from the bigger gash the little creek went into—main Squaw Creek. (How many Squaw Creeks are there?)

I had to get up high first and I took a circuitous route, accompanied by a dog who was showing the wear and tear of a long day by mid-afternoon. I went nearly to the top of one bank of the canyon, caught my breath and listened. There were some calls from behind me and still higher, birds I hadn't noticed earlier and obviously sending signals to the ones I was after. They were a help.

Then came a little chatter from *my* birds across the canyon. There were three outcroppings of rock there and I couldn't tell which one they were in. But I ruefully told myself I at least knew which side of the canyon they were on. All the way down and up the other side, being careful to stay upstream from the birds. I stopped when I *thought* I was above them and within a few minutes they called. I was right. I worked carefully along the face, stopping every few steps.

They didn't say much but finally they gave themselves away with a soft clacking. I had passed them and now I was almost sure which rocks they were in. No more calling now. They knew about me. Cackles from farther up the canyon went unanswered.

So I stood atop a little wedge of rimrock and studied its base below me. Slide rock and thin cheatgrass. There was a tiny movement down there. Only two chukars blew out ten feet beneath me but I couldn't use more and more would have been harder to stalk. When I ordered, "Hunt dead!" I sounded triumphant but my dog was useless, finally standing hopelessly with one foot touching an unseen dead bird. It rained a week later and the dogs came into their own.

The canyon shadows were long but it was still warm and as I headed on down on my way to the trail I stopped briefly and heard a very faint chukar sound far above where I'd made my kills. It was the birds that had been talking to mine earlier and I stared up there for a few moments, not really expecting to see anything, but I did see something, a speck on a boulder, a speck that moved a couple of feet while I watched. The sentry wanted a better position. I didn't turn back. I guess I was just too tired.

There are good chukar dogs and some that should stay with other work. Iron Mike, a hard-boiled ruffian we called a Brittany, was not a chukar dog. Iron Mike, who began life as a street dog and who had been only partly civilized by Ben Williams, looked a little like a Brittany seen through dirty binoculars and must have had a burly setter in his ancestry somewhere. Ben and I were intrigued by the way old Mike would raid a big field of wheat stubble for Huns, going hard downwind of them and then holding them for long periods while we panted toward him.

I tried Mike on chukars. I knew where the birds were all right—approximately. I knew they were in rimrock above a canyon and I didn't know what was back of the rim. I'd seen it only looking up from the canyon where a Jeep trail and my truck went. I figured the only way to get to those birds was to climb up there and get on their level, if not a little above them. I couldn't tell if the slope continued above the rock. Mike and I started up, Mike apparently looking for rabbits or porcupines, having had no introduction to chukars. I climbed for half an hour and when I'd stop to rest I'd hear the chukar sounds but they held no interest for Mike, who investigated what appeared to be a rockchuck hole.

"Hunt close!" I told Mike as we finally got almost to the rimrock with its jutting little sage bushes. It was an idle gesture for the Dow Jones average would have meant just as much to Mike.

I got to the rimrock, crawled through a shattered gap in it and lost track of Mike for a moment. There was a broad flat back of the rock and I was to learn after that it could be reached by truck—a typical chukar hunt discovery—but for the moment my problem was the chukars somewhere along the rim. And Mike suddenly became birdy, setting one big foot carefully ahead of another as he eased along the top.

"Easy! Easy!" I panted in a wobbly chase. Mike moved faster and two chukars stormed out of the rock to plunge down into the canyon—too quick for my gun.

"Whoa!" I yelled. It was a word evidently unknown to Mike. He had never heard it while working garbage cans in the alleys of his youth. It is possible he confused it with "Charge!" or possibly he considered it a sort of universal rebel yell.

I do not like to dwell on what happened next and I am going to state it with composure and as briefly as possible. Mike ran up half a mile of chukars along that Nevada rim. They came off the rocks as smaller and smaller specks as he got farther away and they dived over the edge. Mike came back with a broad grin on his face and I showed remarkable restraint.

"Come on, Mike," I said. "Let's go back to the truck."

I put him in the dog box and took him to the stubble fields.

I have never heard of anyone using poisoned corn or grasshoppers with fishhooks in them, but evidently most other chukar methods have been explored. There were the guys with the sunroof on their four-wheel-drive wagon.

We had a camp within a few feet of the trail used to get into our Idaho chukar country—far enough in that you could hear birds now and then from the camp itself. We worked hard all day and I believe two of us killed six birds. The young guys with the wagon, three of them, came driving out and I asked them how they'd done. We'd seen them cruising the creek roads earlier with a lookout stationed in the sunroof opening, looking like a turret gunner. No doubt about their being road hunters—and maybe they'd even shot birds flushed by the car.

"We got twenty-three," reported one of the group. "Don't hunt them on those hills. Nothing for them to eat up there."

As I pondered this misinformation, Jack Ward scratched his pointer's ears and said he wished I wouldn't ask other people how they were doing. Ruined the whole day, he said. I could tell it really bothered old Jack because he mentioned it several times.

Now Jack has a funny memory that sometimes fixes faces with amazing permanence. He went back to Idaho on another hunt a couple of weeks later.

"I saw one of those guys in a supermarket," Jack reported. "So I asked him if they ground-sluiced those birds. He said of course they had—that anybody climbing around those hills and making them fly was stupid."

Last fall, Fred Terwilliger and I had hunted a lower slope for some time, had apparently chased all of the birds off it, and were attracted by a little depressed groove of sliderock high above. There was frequent calling from there. The area was roughly thirty yards by twenty—something like that—and it was quite steep.

We went up there, huffing and puffing, with a tired dog that was beginning to lose enthusiasm. We went a roundabout way, and when we were about level with the callers a little wad of birds roared around the mountain and down, out of range, apparently coming from near where we'd heard the calls.

"There go our birds!" I complained.

But we'd gone that far, so we kept on climbing, then cut across to where we'd heard the calls earlier, just to make sure we'd really worked it out. After I passed the little groove there were a few birds far ahead but I didn't get a shot. Fred stayed with the little groove and checked it out thoroughly, apparently foot by foot. Then we headed down toward the truck. It rained a little with a sprinkle of sleet.

On the tailgate and tired out, we gulped some coffee and stared back up the slope to where we had been.

"That bunch that flew was our birds all right," I said. "Nothing up there now."

A black cloud moved over our little mountain and the wind shifted a little. Then it came softly, but without mistake, from the little groove with the slide rock.

"Chuk-a-a-a-r, Chuk-a-a-a-r!"

"Would you like some more coffee?" asked Fred.

In more innocent days we used to call all such things "buck fever" although modern psychiatry has more definitive terms. The diagnosis may be explicit but the cures are yet to come.

Call it pressure, and it can build in wondrous ways.

Chapter Twenty

Parting Shots

A lighted cigarette doesn't shoot very well in a skeet gun but one gunner tried it. He'd never broken 100 straight (quite a few haven't) but he was getting close and he was ready for his doubles on Station 7 of the final round. This time he'd played it cool.

He called for the targets, smoked the first one with a smooth swing and then heard a dull snap when he pulled the trigger again.

Bad shell, he thought, and he opened his over-under, only to find one chamber was empty. His golden moment had fled and he was sure he'd loaded that second barrel until he found his cigarette was lying on the ground, still smoking. It seems he'd slid it into the chamber instead of a cartridge.

But then there was the fellow who tried to stuff his glove into his deer rifle while a big buck bounced away, and the other guy who carefully put the empties back into the magazine. He'd missed a deer with several shots but expected it to reappear from a patch of brush and was understandably a bit nervous. I don't know how many deer hunters have sighted their first game and jacked all of their cartridges to the ground unfired.

There are shooters who can hit Lifesavers in the air with a rifle but have missed 15-pound turkey gobblers on the ground at 30 yards with a shotgun.

In more innocent days we used to call all such things "buck fever" although modern psychiatry has more definitive terms. The diagnosis may be explicit but the cures are yet to come.

Call it pressure, and it can build in wondrous ways.

Now on some of those North Florida plantations quail shooting can be pretty formal. If you go with the right people you ride in a rubber-tired shooting wagon with hydraulic brakes, pulled by matched mules. The dog handlers ride

Tennessee walking horses and when the dogs point some-body hands you your gun and tells you where to stand while he flushes the birds with a leather flushing whip. Everybody, including the Labrador retrievers sitting on top of the wagon, is watching and I don't know what term to use in describing the mental state of a green gunner in this atmosphere since "buck fever" is too mild a phrase.

Well anyway, this man hadn't done very much hunting and he was somewhat tensed up when he walked over to where the dog handler was standing, together with the dogs. It was at that moment one of the wagon mules sneezed and the man shot twice. Now I suppose blasting one mule would be con-sidered only a minor breach of etiquette but making a double on mules is highly unusual.

Concentration on game can sometimes divert one's atten-tion from equally important matters. Many years ago I was in charge of a gun-safety program for the Florida Game and Fresh Water Fish Commission. One of my duties was to secure detailed reports of all firearms accidents. Some of the written reports, couched in rather formal language, were mar-vels of understatement, especially those that were recorded by police officers as direct statements from those involved.

Like this:

"The accident occurred in the following manner: You know the scope sight is somewhat above the barrel of a rifle. Well, I was going to take a very long shot and I wanted something to rest my rifle on. I told my friend to lie down on the ground on his stomach and I then laid the rifle across his buttocks, sighting through the scope sight. When I fired I found the barrel of the rifle was shorter than I had thought."

And like this (in response to a question as to why a man with a turkey call had been splattered with Number Fours):

"He was by a tree and he sounded like a turkey."

Hunters in a duck blind are likely to be pretty close to-gether. A shotgun barrel was brought to a gunsmith friend of mine for possible repair. It had been blown off six inches from the muzzle.

"Oh no," the customer said. "It wasn't plugged with dirt. My friend and I got a little mixed up when a bunch of ducks came in and he tried to shoot at my end of the flock. I guess I was pointing at his end."

There are, of course, the stories of new big game hunters who have tried to bring deceased mules through checking stations, complete with shoes: errors in identification rather than the result of nervousness. When I was a kid in Kansas there used to be a rabbit-shaped rock on a hillside which, through the years, was badly worn away by annual fusillades of shot and bullets. One land owner in the East gets a great kick out of hearing bullets whanging off an iron deer in his nearby forest.

But the subtle bits of psychology that undo experienced marksmen delight me more than these more blatant flights of mentality. Years ago I was watching a pistol match in San Francisco. It was rapid fire and it happened that the relay of 40 some shooters was made up of some of the finest pistolmen in the country. The range was located on the shore of a lake.

Rapid fire is five shots in 10 seconds and just after the electric target carriers turned, a mallard hen that was nesting down at the lake shore decided to get out to forage a bit. She flew a foot above the targets from one end of the line to the other. You wouldn't believe some of the scores. I assume the mallard thought the season had opened early that year.

Then there are the deliberate psyching experts such as the skeet or trap shooter involved in a shootoff who totes a whole case of ammunition up to the field to give the impression he's never going to miss. And I once knew a trapshooter and live-pigeon marksman who always used a very expensive Parker trap gun. It was handsomely engraved and the working parts were perfection but the stock was held together by a stovebolt and the entire exterior was carefully rusted to look like something found back of a chicken house. Undoubtedly it had its effects on many shooters with gleaming guns competing for considerable bread.

This same expert would go to great lengths to discombobulate the opposition in any kind of a shootoff. He would feign intoxication, imbecility or both and I once saw him at a little country trapshoot for nothing more expensive than a Thanksgiving ham. He was tied with a state champion and there was to be a shootoff just between the two of them—miss and out.

The guy with the rusty Parker claimed to have lost his ammunition and left the champ standing alone in front of everyone. When they paged him on the loudspeaker he answered in a shout from somewhere back of the clubhouse, stating he had found his green shells but wanted to shoot red shells and would be there in a minute.

When he showed up he apologized profusely. The champ missed the first target, whereupon the tormentor inked one and then suggested in a loud voice that they start over because the champ had encountered a tricky bit of wind and it wasn't fair.

The beaten champion shook his head and walked off. A moment later I heard his car start in the parking lot. Of course he was madder at himself than at the man with the Parker for he was being had. In more formal shoots such antics wouldn't be tolerated and in such cases Rusty Parker would be the soul of propriety, except for the rust on his gun and the fact he blew loudly through his barrel after each shot.

Being a lousy shot myself I've seldom been in a position where psychology could have much effect on somebody else, but I was once the innocent instrument of a fine gunner's embarrassment.

I was going to hunt desert quail and inquired around as to who could show me the ropes. This initiated an involved attempt to job me. A joker friend lined me up with a man noted for marksmanship. He wrote a letter implying that I was a cocky wiseacre who would try to show him up, so the expert was all set to wipe me out. Then, at the last minute the comedian told me of the plot with poorly suppressed giggles, knowing a good shot who was trying to would make me look like even more of a slob than I am.

So I arrived at the scene in a state of cowering apprehension and the day started off with my dog and the expert's dog staging a roaring fight. By that time I hoped we wouldn't even find any quail but we did.

My green dog pointed in an awkward place with hills and brush all around. The birds were scattered and one of them went up like a rocket somewhere behind me. I poked frantically at the shadow that faded into the brush and was amazed to see it fall in a bloom of feathers. Another sailed off from up ahead, swinging back along a hillside, and I somehow knocked it down too. I loaded my double in a daze and stabbed at a third bird whistling up a steep incline. It folded. The expert had not fired a shot yet and a third party commented:

"See what you're up against, Frank?" Of course the amazed hotshot assumed he was the butt of a cruel joke, having been sent forth to compete with one of the world's best, and missed wildly when a bird fluttered up his vest. He finished the day in jumpy frustration. I managed to hide behind bushes and hills and killed a few more carefully selected birds to maintain my precarious reputation. Whew!

A week later, hunting alone, I killed about one for four and concluded that nobody can always be unlucky before an audience.

When I used to shoot pistols I sometimes helped coach police officers. It was a day when there were few organized marksmanship programs in the smaller cities and some rookie police hardly knew how to load their guns. I accepted the invitation of a police training officer (a threadbare title) to help him coach at an indoor range.

Feeling pretty important I arrived at the appointed time and approached the closed range door to find the training officer sitting outside. From within came the thunderous roar of service weapons with heavy loads.

"Okay," I said. "Let's go in and get started."

"Oh no," said the lieutenant. "*You* go in there. I'm not getting in the same room with those lunatics!"

There was this fellow we'll call Lee who suddenly appeared on the competitive shooting scene. Lee was young and co-ordinated and evidently had Freon for blood and he appeared from nowhere to clean up his first slow-fire .22-caliber pistol match. His triumph over some fine gunners made him a bit cocky. Well, let's change that from cocky to impossible.

Lee began practicing at an indoor range which he entered with a swagger and frequently with the announcement that he'd take anybody in a slow-fire match with a .22. Came the evening when a shooter named Dick, not noted for slow-fire excellence, told Lee that he'd beat him for money, marbles or chalk and Lee almost stumbled getting his gun box set up and racking his target down on the trolley.

The match was for only 10 shots and when Lee lost by one point he was sure it was a fluke for it was one of the best scores his opponent had ever fired. He almost stammered as he proposed another go with a bit of financial incentive. He lost that one by a single point too and insisted on a chance to get even. By now his concentration was wavering and he lost by a single point again. Several targets later he paid up, slammed his gun box shut with shaky hands under the polite smiles of onlookers and stalked from the scene.

At that range you fired from soundproofed booths, open at the rear, and as Lee reached the end of the line he heard strangling sounds from one of the compartments and glared into it to see a man lying on the floor writhing in glee. Beside the man was a heavyweight target rifle with a 20-power scope in addition to two spotting scopes—one aimed at the spot where Lee's target had been and one aimed at Dick's target frame. From there, the prone marksman could give Lee's tormentor any score he wanted while Dick fired harmlessly into the backstop without disturbing the target being methodically punched by the target rifle.

Lee went on to become a top competitor but he did it with humility.

Before tranquilizers got in their licks, adrenalin pumpers used to try all sorts of things to calm their screaming nerves and it's an open secret (booze is taboo at most shoots) that alcohol played an important part. One Navy big-bore team with a fine record seemed to be made up of semi-invalids. They arrived at the shoots groggy and silent and I asked their coach about it.

"Oh, that's my system," he said. "I take all of them out the night before the match and get them stinking drunk. I bring them in at dawn and they're too sick to be nervous."

One pistol marksman used alcohol under the supervision of a physician. The eventual dosage was a grisly 3/8 pint of brandy on an empty stomach 12 minutes before a morning match began. It worked pretty well for the dazed victim and he told his friends about it. One of them decided to try it.

After his relay he walked carefully from the line to be met by the more experienced brandy gunner.

"How did it go?" asked the one who had prescribed the dosage.

"Great!" said the new convert thickly. "I shot f-f-four sixes but I didn't give a damn!"

*Somewhere in most detailed books on shotgunnery there
will be a little section of misinformation about snipe,
the only firm ground of agreement being that they are
hard as hell to hit. There are snipe that are hard as
hell to hit and some that are even harder, which has
led to an old rule of mine, less effective since outdoor
littering has become unstylish. My rule was that really
good snipe shooting grounds are not found by looking
for empty shells but by looking for empty shell* boxes.

Chapter Twenty-One

Snipe, Just So

I would like to think there may be some left, missed by the collectors and diligent cleaners. They'd be in undusted old attics or in old barns, possibly back of more modern things in rural closets. It has been some years since a mail order house advertised a few leftover snipe decoys.

I know of no one who still uses such decoys since shorebird shooting is a backwater of shotgunning today. More than ten years ago the editor of one of the big national outdoor magazines told me he wasn't interested in a snipe story.

"Snipe," he said, "are not an 'in' thing."

So the Wilson's snipe or "jacksnipe" is generally ignored, even unrecognized, by hunters of big game, and tiresomely related to the hoary gags concerning youngsters sent with burlap sacks to wait for mysterious creatures in forest darkness. Even some owners of fine shotguns in leather cases are not sure just what a snipe is. They have never heard of a "whisp" of snipe. I spelled it "wisp" once and was taken to task.

Shorebirds were hunted in wheeling swarms a century ago, a time often called the "golden age of shotgunning." It was both commercial and sport shooting and when the fragile waders became scarce through overshooting and habitat destruction shorebird seasons were closed. Many years later someone noticed that snipe were fairly plentiful and it was after World War II that the snipe seasons were reopened, but shorebird hunting had been almost forgotten, a happy condition for those of us who could remember those other snipe seasons.

There had been the plovers and the curlews, some of the local names being a little vague, and there had been the thousands of carved decoys and the recommended tactics like those written of by Captain Adam Bogardus, sometimes involving the judicious use of horses and buggies. I knew one tradition lover who put a bunch of snipe decoys on a gleaming mud flat only a few years ago, but most snipe are walked up.

I was in a goose blind near the shore of a British Columbia lake waiting for the morning flight to leave noisily and hopefully give some pass shooting when a rag-tag flock of small birds came past us, going like rookie flight cadets, apparently with one wing working at a time. Their calls were unmistakable.

"Snipe!" I announced.

"Show me some more," said the Canadian in the blind with me. "I didn't get a good look at the bunch."

"I always wondered what a snipe was," he said when I identified another flight. The Canadian goose hunter was surprised that anyone would shoot anything so small.

There was the snipe story in a national magazine, showing a picture of what I took to be yellowlegs and there was the article in which the author explained that woodcock and jacksnipe were the same thing. There was the time I was sent to a reported snipe hotspot, only to find myself surrounded by legions of killdeers. A duck hunter ran his outboard for some distance to show me some brackish water snipe but although there was a variety of wading birds we saw no snipe.

"All kinds of snipe," he said, and I was too polite to say I couldn't see any at all.

Snipe nest in the North, some of them beyond the Arctic Circle, their migrations having a special appeal as does that of any small gamebird, but they lack the glamour of the woodcock, even though they can outfly it. Woodcock bring forth sentimental prose and pet names. Perhaps it is because a woodcock holds for pointing dogs and because quaking aspen and alder thickets appeal more to men with light double shotguns than do wet flats of mud and weeds. I know of no book written entirely about snipe shooting and snipe gunning runs more to low comedy than to tradition. Perhaps it is better that way for I doubt if the snipe could handle the full-scale onslaught of being an "in" thing.

The courtship music of the woodcock is rapturously re-corded in all sorts of books and articles and men in rubber-bottomed pacs and frayed canvas coats will visit northern woodcock grounds in early spring, waiting breathlessly at dusk to watch the antics of a bird too venerated to be called a comic. Perhaps in stacks of theses in university libraries are detailed accounts of the performances of snipe during nesting season but snipe are generally unnoticed then.

There is a trout stream in Montana, one of those spring creeks with regular insect hatches and gently rising trout, that is bordered by enough marshy ground to serve as a jacksnipe center. Although I fired wildly at hundreds (thousands?) of winter snipe through the years, I did not know what I was hearing for the first few days of fishing. Midsummer.

It was a soft sound that went *whoo-whoo-whoo* and seemed to come from everywhere until I concluded it was almost straight overhead, and I looked up a few times but saw no bird. I went back to my fishing but a few minutes later I saw a snipe sitting on a fencepost—nothing unusual in Montana at that time of year. It must have been the third or fourth day that I learned it was a snipe who made the strange overhead sound—a snipe holding his fluttering position with-out much forward movement and pretty high. High enough that he was a little hard to identify. I don't know how many nest near that creek but I look for them each year now.

Snipe have the wrong wings for upland game birds—long and slender—and their flying is erratic enough to appear amateurish, a balm to the ego of new shooters who always announce sadly they have hit a bird that simply doesn't fall. But the bird's flight is amazingly efficient and when a snipe joins up with a formation of blue-winged teal just for the hell of it, he seems to make no special effort to keep up.

The fact is a snipe seems to do a great many things just for the hell of it—his objectives concealed somewhere in snipe logic. He can form into a feathered arrowhead and dive toward earth from considerable altitude, swerving wildly at the last instant and then landing gently, after which he looks around in what seems to be a mixture of surprise and con-ceit—surprise that he's made it one more time without driving his beak clear to bedrock, and conceit that he has just performed a maneuver that would disable most birds.

He has, of course, a considerable range of flying speeds and a spirit of individualism that crops up regularly in snipe flocks. A dozen or twenty snipe will swing about over a marsh in tight formation in what appears to be a senseless course and then one will suddenly detach himself and do the dive, or simply leave for another marsh. Although there doesn't appear to be a leader in a flock of snipe, I am sure there must be someone in charge and the occasional deserter gets fed up with the program.

Somewhere in most detailed books on shotgunnery there will be a little section of misinformation about snipe, the only firm ground of agreement being that they are hard as hell to hit. There are snipe that are hard as hell to hit and some that are even harder, which has led to an old rule of mine, less effective since outdoor littering has become unstylish. My rule was that really good snipe shooting grounds are not found by looking for empty shells but by looking for empty shell *boxes*. A snipe-seeking associate has gone so far as to say that he preferred Remington shells over Winchesters or Federals for snipe shooting, the reason being that Remington boxes are green and afford better hiding places for snipe in grassy areas.

Within the false information given about snipe shooting is the rule that snipe always call just as they jump, which is not true at all—some of them leave as quietly as owls, often getting at least 50 yards away before giving the call generally written as *Scaipe!* I have written that the word is actually *escape*, but it hasn't caught on among game biologists.

A considerable share of the snipe shooters I interview have done it at some isolated pond where they have been taken by someone who has located the birds considerable distance from the marshland, and the birds mill around for some time before leaving. It is in such places that they "simply drop back to earth after flying a few yards and give you another chance." Not the snipe I chase, not by a damned sight.

On big, open marshes the birds generally go for hundreds

of yards and sometimes for miles before putting in again—unless they are those occasionally tame birds that have somehow avoided hunters. I have occasionally found them quite tame in Canada and the northern United States. In Florida where I have done most of my snipe hunting, the winter snipe tends to be a suspicious fellow. Generally they live on terrain open enough that they can watch you coming and hear your boots clutching the mud.

Walking up snipe is a science. The rule is to walk downwind so they'll show their light undersides as they take off but no authority has explained a return to where you started without walking back through all of that mud again. Geometry indicates that for every downwind walk there must be an upwind walk unless you have someone meeting you with a boat or a swamp buggy.

Since it is essential to sight a bird early in his flight, the best drill is to keep your eyes fixed straight ahead and cover limited area as you walk, trying to ignore raucous *scaipes* from the side—except when a bird waits until you are quite close, in which case you will have time to turn—and miss him with great care.

Always carry a large bandanna for two reasons. Use it to mark the spot where you think a bird has fallen while you search in enlarging circles. I also use it to wipe my sweaty palms and smooth out the checkered pattern on my hands, caused by tightly clutching a shotgun stock for long periods.

I have read that when a snipe jumps you should wait until he quits his "jeeping" and levels out before shooting. This is a fine plan if he gets up at your feet but my snipe generally take the air at a minimum of 15 yards and by the time they quit the erratic part I'd need a telescopic sight. Small shot is necessary for the vital part going away is about the size of a golf ball. I'd use 8½'s or 9-shot.

And while the authorities recommend a "light, open-bored gun," we must check the circumstances. Light, yes, but not always open-bored. When snipe get up wild you need a pretty snug choke or they'll fly right through a pattern.

I am reading here that if you can hit three out of five snipe you needn't be ashamed in any shotgun company. Since I am satisfied with one for three, I would rather not associate with people who kill three out of five. Of course, it depends upon the cover and wildness of the birds. I have done pretty well myself on rare occasions when I find snipe in rather tall cover where I surprise them, and on those rare occasions when they turn back past me to get where I've been. There are detailed plans and diagrams for driving snipe which work fine but I do not like that because I don't want drivers or anybody else watching me when I shoot at snipe.

When you move a bunch and there's something to hide in nearby you can wait for them to come back. The gliding and darting returns are not so tough but when they do the dive it's a different story. I shall not detail methods for hitting diving snipe as I do not recall ever having done it.

A great many snipe are shot along the shore of public water and access isn't always a problem, although much of the good country is best reached by boat. I once located a veritable snipe convention on private pasture land and in a fit of snipe fever I tried to lease a few hundred yards of bog. The owner became suspicious immediately, never having heard of any-one leasing snipe grounds. He was sure I was engaged in some nefarious scheme such as drug smuggling or cattle thiev-ery and his civility deteriorated to obvious animosity. After he flatly refused, I could feel the eyes of him and his hired man boring into my back as I walked away. I think they took down my car license number. Woodcock would have been different.

Last year was the best, partly because the year before was a slow snipe season for me. I don't know if there were fewer snipe the year before but I suspect I simply didn't find the right places. Last year was the best, too, partly because mine has been a long affair with snipe, beginning in Kansas at a place then called Farlington Lake which was an old railroad pond with a strip of tough walking and a snipe or two. My Model-12 Winchester pump was brand new, had cost 46 dol-lars and was full-choked. The snipe were pretty safe, actually safer than the teal and occasional mallards that came to Far-lington Lake from somewhere north of Kansas City and pos-sibly even north of Omaha.

Last year I put the aluminum johnboat in at a Florida ramp, not crowded because that lake hasn't been good fishing lately. It blooms with greenish algae and there aren't many bass at all. In late winter there's generally a raft of diving ducks in the middle and a few blue-winged teal in the weedy little coves but this time I was after snipe. I went out into open water, past a couple of alligators and swung wide from the commercial fishermen's floats. A cloud of the diving ducks and a few gulls went up as I crossed a mile of open water and located myself by an old winter landmark—the gleaming patch of white pelicans on the same point year after year.

The first stop didn't work out. I hiked a quarter mile and a single snipe took off from the short grass where there had been dozens a few years back. There were a few killdeers along that shore. There were more birds at the second stop.

I could see great blue herons, killdeers, jumpy, swinging little flocks of tiny shorebirds and plenty of black birds and a few boat-tailed grackles. Back of the soggy shoreline flat were cattle, humpbacked Brahmans that will never seem American to me. Cattle egrets were pretty well away from the shoreline. The outboard motor bumped mud bottom and I stalled in a patch of hyacinths lodged against dead weeds.

I anchored and got out, wading in six inches of water and four inches of mud toward more solid footing a hundred yards away. A cloud of assorted birds left when I was 25 yards out and I saw snipe among them. It looked good.

The birds were scattered along a mile of shore, generally flushing out of range, but there were chances. I stabbed at one bird, already almost out of range. It was a tentative try and when I tried to follow the gyrating flight I fired at least two feet to one side.

"*Scaipe,*" said the bird I had shot at. "*SCAIPE!*" said another snipe leaving from much closer. I could not locate the nearer one as he skimmed the ground, a brown bird skimming brown, dead grass and dormant hyacinth leaves. I reloaded. Already my palms were damp. Game, I contemplated, can excite you only so much, whether tiger, snipe or record ram. Another snipe flushed, this one going really fast and swinging in a wide curve. *Scaipe!*

Somehow this time the muzzle went right and swung ahead

what seemed too far. The bird folded instantly, spatting and bouncing where half an inch of water covered the ground. A single feather floated down and another snipe left but I never took my eyes from where my prize had fallen. When I had found it and smoothed the feathers the way woodcock shooters do I missed three birds straight—but I still had a long day ahead.

When I went back to the boat I had a treasured little bundle of snipe in my vest and an embarrassingly large pocket full of empty shells. The low sun shone on a contrail pointed toward Orlando and a formation of white ibis crossed a yellow cloud edge.

"How'd you do?" asked the young guy at the ramp. "They bitin'?"

"I was just hunting snipe," I said as I have explained a hundred times. I stowed the gun in the wagon.

"Lemme see 'em," he prodded, looking suspicious.

I opened the little plastic bird box with the ventilation holes and he peered in.

"Why those are little *birds!*" he said.

Yep.

Everyone knows it is the in thing to sneak new shot-
guns past wives. Anyone who doesn't do that simply
isn't with our crowd. We know that, don't we? The
snuck-in shotgun is as much a part of real America as
the filthy fishing hat.

Chapter Twenty-Two

Gun Running

I have never gotten very far in this outdoor business because hunting and fishing people are long on tradition and we can't seem to get anything like that started at our house.

Whereas new fishing tackle is something a true sportsman is supposed to sneak past his wife, my wife must be steered around the better tackle shops. Her special weakness is fly rods and 34 are more than we really need, especially since we aren't collectors. Each has been purchased because it was expected to do a better job than the last one.

The fly rod business came to a head, so to speak, when Debie found one she didn't know about.

"This is a fine custom job," Debie said. "Somehow we have gotten it in with our stuff. It is evidently a steelhead rod—or maybe for light salt water—and it has special guides. It must be expensive. Who could it belong to?"

That was when the fly rod business slowed down because I explained to Debie that she was displaying a rod she'd once had made as the end-all, be-all of Number Eight fly rods. We've saved considerable in the tackle department since then. This leads me right into the shotgun-broker business.

Everyone knows it is the in thing to sneak new shotguns past wives. Anyone who doesn't do that simply isn't with our crowd. We know that, don't we? The snuck-in shotgun is as much a part of real America as the filthy fishing hat. Those who haven't snuck in a shotgun or two and told about it where their wives won't hear about it just don't have the feel for woodsmoke, good bourbon and bird dogs. Now this shotgun-broker business:

You buy ordinary shotguns in general sporting goods stores, hardware stores and even department stores. But when you want a British side-by-side bird gun with unobtrusive scroll engraving and a straight grip, you generally go to a specialist. These are sometimes called "gun brokers." They sell largely by correspondence and they keep shipping guns around by registered mail. I know one of them pretty well. He was a sort of amateur broker with no showroom at all but he made his headquarters at a local sporting goods store and he kept getting guns through the mail. After inspecting them he'd buy some and send the others back. He had a pretty big phone bill and these guns ranged from some of those super-engraved and inlaid Italian pieces to some of the better old Americans. For one period he was looking at several Parkers a week.

I'm no collector but sniffing fine shotguns is a habit of mine and from time to time he'd ask my opinion of something fresh out of the morning mail. There were Purdeys, Holland & Hollands, Westley Richards's, Merkels and so on, almost the gamut of fine guns. It reached the point where I could be critical of any of them. Before long I could whip up a Famars that cost more than a Lincoln Continental, glance down the hand-filed rib and announce that it was too muzzle heavy or that the stock was too long or too straight. I got pretty blasé about the whole thing and I was pretty frank with my opinions.

"Bird guns," I explained to my friend, who seemed to be hanging on every word, "should be short and light and I like twelve gauge because I point them better than twenties. The extra bulk (not weight) is an aid to pointing. And I sort of like boxlocks instead of sidelocks because I think they're a little harder to wreck if you fall down a hill with one, even if they don't cost as much and don't have as much room for engraving. And I like about a quarter-inch castoff. And all of this can be had at less than six-and-a-half pounds for light twelve-gauge loads."

This little speech was repeated with minor variations pretty regularly and sometimes a store visitor would tune me in and listen to me as if I were an authority, all of which made me feel pretty good.

Then, believe it or not, my friend the amateur gun broker began to show me slightly less expensive guns that looked a little like what I liked and I saw that I had convinced him, which made me more and more free with my observations.

One day he unwrapped a William Powell, which was made in Birmingham, England and he had the short barrels and light weight. The stock was English style and it was a box-lock. It wasn't nearly as expensive as most of the guns he had been showing me but it wasn't likely to show up in a cut-rate hardware store either. He'd been getting closer and closer to that one all the time.

"Now," I said, "you have moved into my alley. This is what a bird gun should be. I could shoot with that."

The amateur gun broker smiled and a couple of eaves-droppers who had come in to buy duck loads listened as if they were hearing something that should be cut in stone. I went over to the post office and then headed home. The Powell had beaten me there.

"You needed an English shotgun," Debie said, "but we had a hell of a time finding what you wanted."

Dogs and people approach things a little differently.
For example, I am very fond of pizza but have never
had a desire to roll in it. Rolling in more or less
odorous things may be somewhat mysterious but I as-
sume the idea is to collect a choice odor and take it
along.

Chapter Twenty-Three

Roller Derby

Dogs are in the smell business. For example, an odor that can immobilize an over-sensitive human can be exhilarating to a dog.

A dog has what I shall call a broad odor-appreciation range. For example, let's take a silky-eared English setter who can smell a woodcock on the other side of a bush which contains a family of field mice, two old bird nests and a dead weasel. Here we have a sensitive creature with true odor appreciation.

Now while seeking a woodcock or quail smell this setter comes upon a raccoon which has been dead for 11 warm autumn days. Reluctant to leave this treasure trove of olfactory delight, the setter hurriedly rolls on it before going on with his hunting. Then, by accident, he finds an irritable skunk and investigates it. After rubbing some of the results of this encounter from his eyes he continues seeking the scent of woodcock or quail. At this point his master questions the old bird hunter's rule of always working a dog upwind but the day is still young.

While happily loping along with his aura of deceased raccoon and living skunk the setter winds a covey of quail and comes to what we shall call a "classic point" from a distance of 30 feet, scenting the quail through heavy wiregrass and a little broom sedge which contains a gopher tortoise. The gunner comes up and, holding his breath briefly because he approaches downwind from the setter, he walks into the covey of quail and shoots one of them with an expert swing of his twelve-gauge improved cylinder and modified Holland & Holland, using a one-ounce load of Number 8 shot. (Even in these hypothetical situations I like to maintain accuracy as to detail.)

The bird falls some distance from and out of sight of the setter, who begins hunting dead and finds it where it has fallen beside a rotting log with the discarded skin of a corn snake draped over it. On the way back to his owner the setter scents a sleeper that did not flush with the other quail, and after blowing a wing feather of the dead quail from his nostrils he makes another classic point. The hunter shoots this bird and the setter tries to retrieve both of them but drops one. By now I believe you follow me in the matter of selective scenting and odor appreciation. Of course the setter is offended that he is put in the kennel that night and not allowed to sleep by the fireplace, despite the insistence of my old hunting friend that setters should be kept by fireplaces, even in warm weather, for aesthetic purposes.

Dogs and people approach things a little differently. For example, I am very fond of pizza but have never had a desire to roll in it. Rolling in more or less odorous things may be somewhat mysterious but I assume the idea is to collect a choice odor and take it along. Still, there is something else about it I can't put my finger on. For example, a dog that has smelled as nearly like a rose as a dog can smell for most of his life is likely to go on a roll when accompanied by another dog he wishes to impress.

Like the time we took Tex on the trout fishing trip with our friends who had a new car. We even debated taking the gleaming car but decided we'd be nowhere that it could get scratched, even though we were going into a Western pasture—with Tex the Brittany and our friend's dog of impeccable poodle ancestry. The pasture was well occupied by Angus cattle and as soon as we opened the door Tex climbed out and showed that coiffed poodle how a real he-dog handles a cow pasture. I got him fairly clean but I had to do it in a pretty cold trout stream and without soap.

But up to now this has been just so much padding to get to a report on the rolling aptitudes of the Duchess of Doonesbury, my 62-pound English pointer. Until I met the Duchess I had paid little attention to the techniques of rolling, considering it a routine move, like sitting down or scratching. The Duchess changed all that.

I trust you have observed rolling. A dog making a serious roll on or in something that smells puts his nose to the ground just a little before he gets to the object. He then sort of slides his nose and the side of his head up alongside it and slowly rolls so that his shoulders strike the optimum spot, whereupon he flops over, momentarily out of control, and then wriggles carefully with his feet in the air. Since he soon acquires the aroma of the rolled-on object I have always wondered why it is that after he stands up concluding the process and shakes himself he then turns to the target and takes another long sniff.

Anyway, that is the pattern of the routine roll for something that smells a little or a great deal. It had never occurred to me that it required any special technique and the matter of accuracy had not come up in my experience until we acquired Dutch. I soon learned that she took rolling seriously but that she was remarkably inaccurate. This came up for the first time when I kicked off my hunting boots and socks and was preparing to head for the shower and heard a scraping sound. It was Dutch endeavoring to roll on my socks but missing them by a good 18 inches. As time went on I realized she had a serious problem with her rolling, having a misunderstanding of rolling trajectory and failing to lead her target properly, thus ending up rolling some distance away. A few days later she tried to roll on my shoes (evidently for practice) when I was wearing them and sitting in a lounge chair. She ended up partly under the chair with her tail caught in a complex mechanism that allows a chair passenger to lie back with his feet up.

Our dogs are generally barred from the bathroom but in a little shack we live in while hunting we cannot conveniently make the bathroom off limits. One evening I heard strange sounds from there and Debie told me it was Dutch with the bath towels. I jumped to my feet and started that way but Debie said not to worry.

"She's been doing this pretty regularly," Debie said. "She pulls the towels of the racks and tries to roll on them but doesn't seem to hit them. No hurry about going in there as they're already on the floor and she won't roll on them."

Shortly afterward, Dutch appeared in the bathroom door and glared at me but I did not laugh.

In approaching a rolling target Dutch's eyes take on a calculating stare and she gathers herself for the effort, measuring distances and seeking the proper foot placement. She lowers her head with clocklike precision and becomes tense in anticipation. I watched his many times and, assured that persistent practice would succeed, I guess I lost interest. But rolling is important.

It was early season in grouse country, warm sun and a long day. Dutch had done her best but there weren't many birds and I was mentally measuring my way to the truck as I stumbled out of a dense patch of aspen and listened for Dutch's bell. I hadn't heard it for a couple of minutes. As I broke from the aspen into open pastureland, I froze in despair.

Two hundred yards away, its presence heralded by a breeze-borne whiff, even from that distance, was a dead cow. And visible too were Dutch's legs, pointed skyward and waving in the snappy, jerky pattern of a dog's luxurious roll in super smell.

I screamed before I had sense enough to blast on my whistle and before me flashed the long ride home in a Ford Bronco with Dutch and her treasured carrion. Finally, Dutch heard me, the waving legs stopped and at last she stood up and ran toward me. Did you call, boss?

Averting my face, I waited until she was at my feet, and holding my breath I gradually turned to eye her. But I needn't have worried. Dutch missed the cow.

There was the prized palomino colt slaughtered by antelope hunters in some distant year, and his ghost haunts a thousand hopeful souls in blaze orange jackets who approach unfriendly ranch gates. He is mourned as much as Custer. And although there is no question that horsemen have had their mounts shot from under them by myopic or hysterical gunners, such stories have been repeated so often that the allegedly unhorsed victims would make up an infantry battalion of trudging saddle-toters.

Chapter Twenty-Four

Season's Greetings

"She's a nice dog," the foreman's wife said. "She wouldn't bother you at all if she didn't have pups."

The lady dog in question had a firm grip on Jack Ward's right leg and since it was too late to retreat, Jack kicked gently and tentatively. Finally, the lady dog let go and returned to wherever she had come from, sounding a little like feeding time at the zoo.

"No," the foreman's wife said. "We don't allow any hunting at all. We have an agreement with the owners."

It was the Double-U, one of those immense Montana ranches owned by out-of-staters and noted for a dim view of hunters. A large share of its neat metal no-hunting signs have been perforated by riflemen—a vandalistic expression of frustration that undoubtedly makes the owners more adamant. Before the Double-U bought them out the smaller ranchers used to let us into that country any time. We used the private land only for access to National Forest.

"Well," said Jack, limping back to the truck, "I guess it didn't hurt to ask."

"On second thought . . ." he mumbled, nursing his wounded leg.

Not that I begrudge the landowner a right to close his property or to assess the appearance and personality of those he does allow to hunt or cross his land, but things are changing in the West. Anyone bent on seeking hunting permission had best plan a careful campaign.

"You better ask to hunt," one youngish friend told me. "My hair is kind of long."

My old hunting buddy, Red Monical, stayed in the truck while I approached several miles of ranch owners during pheasant season. Red had new brush pants and they had a decidedly pink cast. I don't want anybody with pink pants

205

approaching a rancher. By next season, Red's pants were acceptable.

Even with careful planning there are awkward moments. A friend of mine walked up to a ranch house door to inquire about Hungarian partridge hunting. He'd left his Brittanies in the car, but one squeezed unseen through a partly opened window.

The rancher at the door seemed preoccupied and stared over Ben's shoulder.

"Oh, I guess it's all right for you to hunt," he said. "But I think you should tell your dog to put down my duck."

That worked out all right, but some years back in another state Max Stevenson didn't do so well. His dog, always soft-mouthed, proudly brought him a barnyard chicken, and in a flurry of embarrassment Max put down the slightly ruffled hen, scolded his dog and switched her a little.

"That was it," muses Max. "From that day on she never retrieved another bird."

I have been embarrassed by some over-tolerant landowners who managed to make me feel like a criminal for even asking, even though they gave me permission.

I walked up to the big ranch house and was met at the door by a friendly face atop ranch clothing. The man was elderly.

"Come on in and sit down," he said. "I'm watching the football game.

"You'll find the pheasants along that creek south of the corrals and clear up toward the bench. Lots of deer in there, too, if you like that kind of hunting. Bring some of your friends next time."

By way of conversation I asked if he had many hunters. "Oh, yes. Lots of hunters. Most of them pretty nice folks. Oh, I've had a few cows shot through the years, but nothing serious. The antelope hunters are the worst. They get excited. Last year they shot through the kitchen, but there was no one in there so it didn't do much damage."

At that point I produced an asinine remark about football, tried to make myself invisible and left quietly.

There is, of course, no secret about outrages performed by hunters through ignorance, carelessness or even vandalism, but some of the more colorful episodes are rich in antiquity and have come down to us as a sort of rancher's folklore.

There was the prized palomino colt slaughtered by antelope hunters in some distant year, and his ghost haunts a thousand hopeful souls in blaze orange jackets who approach unfriendly ranch gates. He is mourned as much as Custer. And although there is no question that horsemen have had their mounts shot from under them by myopic or hysterical gunners, such stories have been repeated so often that the allegedly unhorsed victims would make up an infantry battalion of trudging saddle-toters. And the deceased and steel-shod mule that is said to have been presented at a game department check station has been placed in so many localities that I half expect to see him hauled in just ahead of me whenever I approach such an installation.

There are, of course, the wrecked gates and cut fences viewed by officers of the law, and there was one rancher who reported such things annually and asked for investigation by authorities.

"George doesn't lie about those fences," said a neighbor. "He cuts them himself."

Why should he do that? For a more obvious reason than you'd suspect. Like many others jealous of their property, he wants to be a good guy in the eyes of his community and he wants a real reason for refusing hunters.

Things have changed. The hunters and the tourists have become *dudes* instead of visitors who should be made welcome.

I am trying to help you. Ever since I tried to sell encyclopedias door to door during the Great Depression I have had the utmost respect for detailed sales programs, and the overcoming of anticipated objections is a major factor. Much of the research undertaken in the West will apply to other parts of the country.

There is something special about Montana because it has only recently attracted enough hunters to put the landowners on their guard. A few of the refusals still come from amateurs, nice people who haven't been reduced to the simple, impregnable "NO." They feel they must give reasons and they have plenty.

Between Lewistown, pheasant capital of the area, and the Missouri Breaks to the north, Marcus Crosby and I did our best one pleasant fall day. On other occasions we managed to get on and had good hunting, but we failed that time and were forced to abandon our Hungarian partridge and pheasant ambitions and settle for sage grouse after being turned away from 50 miles of ranches. Bless the sage hens because they (and some sharptails) live happily on the yellow squares of the map—Bureau of Land Management Land. You soon learn that government-owned ground is a bit short on garden spots and long on dusty arroyos and sagebrush. Sight a fertile creek-bottom and you'll find it's private property, even when it's only a narrow streak on your map.

If you decide to ask permission for private property, you must forego set approaches. Given what you hope is the proper apparel (hunting clothes not too clean and not too dirty), you must probe cautiously.

Don't spout that your well-trained dogs prevent the escape of cripples.

"I'll let you hunt, but leave those dogs in your truck," the man said. "I've got cattle in there."

Admittedly there have been bird dogs that chased cows but many ranchers confuse Brittanies and setters with starved grey wolves.

"I let no one hunt with dogs," the rancher said. "I wouldn't care how many Huns or prairie chickens (sharptail grouse) you kill, but dogs scare our pheasants."

"I'm against the use of dogs," the rancher said. "I believe in giving the birds a chance."

The preference of one species over another can be mystifying.

"You can hunt big chickens (sharptails and sage hens) but leave the little chickens (Hungarian partridge) alone. They don't hurt anybody."

"You can hunt those little Huns but don't bother anything else. We want to keep our *real* gamebirds."

"You can hunt that other stuff now, but when the pheasant season opens we're going to close 'er up."

And the pleas of scarcity . . .

"We don't have any pheasants any more," the rancher said sadly, ignoring the persistent cackling of a ringneck cock in his brush shelterbelt. "The foxes cleaned them out."

And nobody denies that foxes kill pheasants, although the hundred-and-some pheasant wings allegedly found at the fox's den years ago have become standard evidence, the location of the den being placed over much of the West and the find being updated annually. Scarcities are also blamed on plenitude of eagles, raccoons, coyotes, skunks and bobcats.

There are the weather reasons. On the day after torrential rains one rancher said the entire valley had been closed because of dry weather.

"But it's muddy now," he hastened to add. "We don't want any hunting after a rain."

Admittedly, too many western hunters do too much driving in hunting territory, feeling that owners of four-wheel-drive vehicles have permanently overcome the discomforts of walking. Protestations that you want to walk instead of ride are frequently unheard. You're simply not believed.

One insurmountable obstacle is the political closing. We have met ranchers who had closed their land to bird hunting because coyote poisoning was illegal. Thousands of square miles of country have been locked because the pheasant limit included a legal hen, and then when the hens became illegal it was left closed to "let the birds come back."

But one of the toughest obstacles to access is psychology. My own. A dozen refusals, to matter how polite, can give me a mental block. I envy the attitude of my friend George, a big personable young guy with a huge grin and an efficient setter. George says you can't lose 'em all and approaches the project with the attitude of the old-time door-to-door magazine salesman. Make a lot of calls, George says, and you'll get results.

"That draw looks great," George would say. "Pull in here."

I watch George talk to the rancher's wife. He comes back with his big grin still intact, but no luck.

"Try that big house."

He comes back with the grin again.

"That guy in there says there aren't any pheasants. Try the next one."

Busy man at the barn. I watch him and George waving their arms amiable.

"He says the pheasants are all hunted out, but we can try if we want to. Should be no problem."

Ten minutes later the first rooster goes up near where we've parked the truck. George folds it. We get a couple more.

"That's enough for here. Let's drive around a little."

We see several roosters in a hayfield.

"Stop at the house."

No problem. Maybe it's George's looks. I have been studying my mirror lately.

I examine the signs on posted property, probably much more carefully than did the ranchers who put them there.

There is the simple *No Trespassing* card, probably picked up as an afterthought at the feed store in town. Then there are the nastily worded ones like:

No Trespassing! Survivors Will Be Prosecuted (calling up images of hard-eyed fence riders armed with Winchesters).

No Fishin', No Huntin', No Trepassin', No Nothin'! (sounds like an arrogant comedian who enjoys turning you away).

Then there's:

No Hunting Without Permission (the most friendly warning of all, although it's generally impossible to learn on short notice who the owner is or where he lives).

Keep Out (smeared on a wooden rectangle with thick paint, evidently by an angry man who couldn't wait to buy a sign).

Keep Out. There Is No Hunting On Either Side Of This Road From Here On (cooperative closing).

KEEP OUT. This land Patrolled Regularly From the Air. (by bombers?)

But the parentheses are products of my imagination. Perhaps the landowners are really friendly people pestered by too many hunters and kindly enough if the approach is polite.

And just before hunting season opens there are the ads placed in local newspapers, describing closed areas, some of them businesslike and some of them giving logical reasons for closing.

But some of those space purchasers get a bit carried away once the buyer is confronted by blank paper and a pen and he vengefully indicts all hunters, all conservation agencies and all political parties which he does not support. And he may end with: "If you don't know where this land is, you better find out. We intend to defend ourselves!"

Things like that.

If you've come from a distance, haven't read the local paper and ask to hunt, the advertiser may castigate you for being illiterate. George would grin at him.

No one denies the hunting criminals, a burden we all must bear, but not all ranchers are honest. There is the *No Trespassing* sign placed on open government land, the dynamited Forest Service culvert and the spirit of ownership acquired by someone who grazes livestock on government grass. People are people.

I don't mean to sabotage license sales. There still is much open hunting available. This permission business was getting out of hand.

It may very well be true that you have to poke around a little harder these days, but if some of the characters I have met in years gone by are any indication, there will always be people to whom hunting is the rule.

It was 15 years ago when I pulled into the service station with a truck full of camping gear. I had never seen the attendant before. He had watched some six gallons of gas go into my tank when he asked me if I were going hunting and I said I was. Before 14 gallons had gone in (30-some cents a gallon) he asked me if I'd like to hunt with him.

I asked if he were a professional guide.

"Oh, no," he said, "but we've got a camp on Freezeout Mountain and we'd sure like to show you some elk if you have the time."

Honest.

And the other service station from which I looked upward to the white tips of the Crazy Mountains. There were mountain goats there and I thought I'd like to have a look at them. How far was it?

"You can drive to within about seven miles of those goats," the man said. "Then you'll need horses."

"Horses are something I don't happen to have with me," I said, being clever.

"Oh, I have horses," he said. "Take them."

I asked him about charges and he was a little hurt.

"Won't cost you anything," he said. "My horses are just standing around eating grass."

This shook me, but I had to say something. I said I didn't know how I'd get the horses to the rough country.

"Oh, take my stock truck," he said. "I'm not using it."

By that time my tank was full and I muttered something about hiking to the goat country, which we did. Borrowing a truckful of horses from a fellow I'd known for four minutes was a little steep.

Kelly made his living pointing things like quail, Huns and ruffed grouse. Pheasant hunting was his hobby, a pursuit requiring a different approach—part trailing, part pointing, part stealth and even a bit of flushing. About pheasants Kelly had his own procedures, methods he had researched and which were unrelated to the procedures of dog-training manuals. Follow Me!

Chapter Twenty-Five

Going Up
Under the Mountain

The pheasants live along the little creeks and in the ragged notches of rimrock above and below the benches where there are miles of wheat stubble in pheasant season. The land goes upward in erratic stairsteps to Montana's Crazy Mountains, and from a great distance there is little sign of the series of gullies, foothills, flats and ranch homes between the main highways and the abrupt piles of the mountains themselves.

From the Yellowstone Valley the scene is compressed as if with a telephoto lens. On a hazy day the various levels are vaguely separated but on bright days the distance shrinks, and it is hard to believe that a man once wrote a book about his life between the highway and the peaks, a busy life in which he lived in several different homes, rode miles of range and had neighbors he seldom saw.

There is more than enough land against the Crazies for a small dog to hunt a lifetime and never meet the same pheasant twice. It really isn't very good pheasant country anyway and old Kelly hunted sharptail grouse, Hungarian partridge and blue grouse there as well.

He hunted there every year of his life, although he lived far away in Florida, and he poked his orange speckled nose into cover from Mexico to northern Alaska while I indulged in the probably childish project of shooting every major upland gamebird of North America over the same Brittany. Kelly must have wondered about that as he plunged off a cliff into an opaque Alaska fog to find a hard-hit ptarmigan, and when he was carried back to the truck in Arizona, helplessly fettered by unfamiliar cholla cactus.

Kelly's furious drive kept me in constant introspection. After several days of hunting was it better to allow a limping, bloody-footed little warrior back into the field or was it better to shut him in the dog box where he wept so that my day was ruined as well as his?

He had already pointed his North American list when Jack Ward and I went up under the mountains late in that pheasant season. It was sunny but there were patches of snow along the willowed creek that bordered the grain.

Kelly loafed in the back of the old Scout until we turned off the asphalt, and then he became a panting sentry, one window to another. He'd sighted a lot of birds from that old truck.

We went up the climbing gravel road that became narrower in a few miles, and we went through the wire gate we'd used for years and across the little creek where there were ruffed grouse sometimes and always darting little brook trout. We parked near the wheatfield and while I dug out the snagged vest and the over-under with the bluing worn I looked up at the Crazies, snowy now that late fall had really come, and looking no nearer than they had when we left the highway miles back.

"We'll work down through these patches of cattails," Jack said, and told of the big ranch dog that had smashed those cattails for him when he was much younger and lived under the mountains.

I released Kelly with the wince I always gave at his reck-less, headlong charge for cover, and he went into the strand of cattails in a series of bounces, visible only at the top of the leaps. There were small, irregular patches of ice among the cattails, carrying old snow, and some of them showed pheasant tracks.

Kelly made his living pointing things like quail, Huns and ruffed grouse. Pheasant hunting was his hobby, a pursuit requiring a different approach—part trailing, part pointing, part stealth and even a bit of flushing. About pheasants Kelly had his own procedures, methods he had researched and which were unrelated to the procedures of dog-training manuals. Follow Me!

We killed only two birds that day and I remember little of the first gleaming cock except that I missed and Jack killed it. It was only a little later that Kelly was working another bird.

He was out of sight part of the time in the narrow jungle but could be seen with his eyes big and his nose flared in the open spots, so we knew the bird was running. The brindle detective went through more cattail patches and through the bank of wild rosebushes and between tight clumps of willows. We followed so far that we wondered if there were other birds to confuse the trail and I began to look at the banks of the draw far ahead, for there have been times when worried old roosters have abandoned the tight cover to scurry, head down, up a gully's shoulders to hide in little notches above where the hunter passes.

Then Kelly left the bottom and turned up the steep bank where the browning grass was almost knee deep. Apparently there had been too much for the cattle that year.

I hurried behind and to one side and he gave me conspiratorial glances of approval. He stopped and pointed and when I reached his side he broke and went on at another angle. Finally he held, his head very high but turning slowly, and I stopped beside him, not knowing which direction to take.

Then, from some page of his pheasant notebook, Kelly drew one of his special tricks. He jumped high in the air three times right beside me, and Kelly's last pheasant left from 20 feet away, startled by the orange and white explosion.

I have remembered the bird as it has hung in the air ever since, the mountain in the background, and the gun going up evenly. The bird came down hard, leaving a few feathers where it had been, but in my mind it hangs forever, climbing toward the Crazies with the muzzle coming up behind it. And while it goes I can see Kelly jumping straight up and down beside me, for part of the game is to make running pheasants fly.

It was an hour later that Kelly did not check in on time. I knew he had worked into a widened tangle farther down the little creek, so I went after him, using my whistle, and I saw him coming laboriously and dazed, a front shoulder smashed and the leg dragging. Finally, a reckless battle with some clump of vines or windfalls had been too much.

I carried him to the truck and laid him on the ground to fix a bed for him in the back, and Kelly's old friend Jack stood helplessly and took a long time to unload his gun. When I turned to lift the little dog into the truck he had crawled several feet, his feverish eyes fixed upon a clump of brush a few yards away. A good place for pheasants.

Weakened by his injury, old Kelly died before the next season began and we buried him under a modest sign that lists the birds he pointed. And once I dreamed of his brindle ghost hurrying along a hill in Alaska and through a Florida swamp, and then in brilliant relief across a ridge below the Crazies.

But the last pheasant is always there, hanging in suspended motion, with the benches, the distant pines, the streaks of yellow stubble and the mountains in the background.